S0-AFD-187

From Colonies to a Country

1635–1790

DEBATABLE ISSUES
IN U.S. HISTORY

VOLUME ONE

From Colonies to a Country

1635–1790

GREENWOOD PRESS
Westport, Connecticut · London

Library of Congress Cataloging-in-Publication Data

Debatable issues in U.S. history / by Creative Media Applications.
      p. cm.—(Middle school reference)
   Includes bibliographical references and index.
ISBN 0–313–32910–9 (set : alk. paper)—ISBN 0–313–32911–7 (v. 1 : alk. paper)—
ISBN 0–313–32912–5 (v. 2 : alk. paper)—ISBN 0–313–32913–3 (v. 3 : alk. paper)—
ISBN 0–313–32914–1 (v. 4 : alk. paper)—ISBN 0–313–32915–X (v. 5 : alk. paper)
    1. United States—History—Miscellanea—Juvenile literature.
2. United States—Politics and government—Miscellanea—Juvenile literature.
3. United States—Social conditions—Miscellanea—Juvenile literature.
4. Critical thinking—Study and teaching (Middle school)—United States.
[1. United States—History. 2. United States—Politics and
government.] I. Creative Media Applications. II. Series.
E178.3.D35   2004
973—dc22   2003056802

British Library Cataloguing in Publication Data is available.

Library of Congress Catalog Card Number: 2003056802
ISBN: 0–313–32910–9 (set)
         0–313–32911–7 (vol. 1)
         0–313–32912–5 (vol. 2)
         0–313–32913–3 (vol. 3)
         0–313–32914–1 (vol. 4)
         0–313–32925–X(vol. 5)

First published in 2004

Greenwood Press, 88 Post Road West, Westport, CT 06881
An imprint of Greenwood Publishing Group, Inc.
www.greenwood.com

Printed in the United States of America

The paper used in this book complies with the Permanent Paper Standard issued by the
National Information Standards Organization (Z39.48–1984).

10 9 8 7 6 5 4 3 2 1

A Creative Media Applications, Inc. Production
Writer: Michael Burgan
Design and Production: Fabia Wargin Design
Editor: Matt Levine
Copyeditor: Laurie Lieb
Proofreader: Pamela Lyons
Indexer: Nara Wood
Associated Press Photo Researcher: Yvette Reyes
Consultant: Mel Urofsky, Professor Emeritus of History at Virginia Commonwealth University

Photo credits:
© Hulton Archives/Getty Images *pages* 6, 8, 11, 15, 19, 21, 24, 26, 31, 35, 36, 51, 59, 62, 64,
69, 72, 77, 79, 84, 86, 96, 99, 108, 127
© Bettmann/CORBIS *pages* 41, 46, 54, 57
© CORBIS *page* 48
AP/Wide World Photographs *pages* 91, 100, 103, 113, 118, 121, 123, 132

Contents

Open debate among its citizens is one of the most important characteristics of a democratic nation like the United States. If citizens did not have the opportunity to express their ideas freely, their leaders would have no way of knowing what issues were important to them.

Introduction

When people come together in a community, they face important decisions about how to run their affairs. Since everyone does not think alike, have the same feelings, or share the same interests, disagreements often arise over key issues.

In a democratic society such as the United States, public debate helps leaders decide what action to take on the most important issues. The debates might start in Congress or another branch of the government. They are often carried on in the media, and they continue in homes, in offices, and wherever concerned citizens gather.

How much power should the national government have?

The five volumes of *Debatable Issues in U.S. History* look at some of the most important issues that have sparked political and social debates, from colonial times to the present day. Some of the issues have been local, such as the dispute between Roger Williams and the Puritan leaders of Massachusetts. Williams struggled to introduce the idea of religious freedom in a community that wanted just one kind of religious worship. Other issues—segregation, for example—had special significance for a large group of people. African Americans, who had once been forced to live in slavery, had to endure lingering prejudice even when they received their freedom during and after the Civil War (1861–1865). Some of the most important issues have touched all Americans, as the country's leaders considered whether to go to war in times of international crisis. The 2003 war in Iraq is just the latest example of that debate.

Throughout American history, certain types of issues have appeared over and over. The details may change, but Americans continue to argue over such things as: How much power should the national government have? How does society balance personal freedom with the need to protect the common good? Which political party has the best vision for strengthening the country? Who should America choose as its friends and its enemies around the world?

> How does society balance personal freedom with the need to protect the common good?

Historians have debated the importance of certain events for hundreds of years. New facts emerge, or interpretations change as the world changes. From the historians' view, almost any issue is debatable. This series, however, focuses on the events and issues that Americans debated as they occurred. Today, few people would question whether the American colonies should have declared their independence from Great Britain; it seems almost impossible to imagine anything else happening. However, to the Americans of the day, the issue was not so clear-cut. Colonial leaders strongly disagreed on what action to take in the months before Thomas Jefferson wrote the Declaration of Independence.

Debate over important issues has always been a vital component of life in the United States. In fact, the very formation of the nation took place amid intense debate over radical new ideas about government. Some of these debates get resolved and become part of history, while others rage on over the decades and even centuries.

At times in the past, debate over key issues might have been limited. From the seventeenth century through most of the nineteenth century, transportation and communication were primitive compared with today. Still, through letters, sermons, newspapers, and government documents, opposing ideas were shared and debated. The lack of electronic communication did not weaken the passion with which people held their beliefs and their desire to shape public issues.

Today, the Internet and other forms of digital communication let millions of people debate crucial issues that face the United States. Better technology, however, does not make it easier for people to settle these issues. As *Debatable Issues in U.S. History* shows, strong emotions often fuel the discussions over the issues. At times, those emotions spill out in violence. On issues that matter most, people are often unwilling to give in, modify their views, or admit that they are wrong. Those attitudes can lead to debates that last for generations. Abortion was a heated issue in 1973, when the U.S. Supreme Court ruled that a woman could legally have an abortion if she chose. Abortion remains a divisive issue today, and there is not much chance that the debate will end.

> Who should America choose as its friends and its enemies around the world?

Debates and disagreements can make it hard for governments to function smoothly. Still, debate allows Americans to explore all sides of an issue. Debate can also lead to new and better ideas that no one had considered before. U.S. Supreme Court Justice William Brennan once noted that Americans have "a profound national commitment to the principle that debate on public issues should be uninhibited, robust, and wide open." That commitment first took shape in colonial America, and it continues today.

A Note to the Reader

The quotations in Debatable Issues in U.S. History *are taken from primary sources, the writings and speeches of the people debating the important issues of their time. Some of the words, phrases, and images in these sources may be offensive by today's standards, but they are an authentic example of our past history. Also, some of the quotes have been slightly changed to reflect the modern spelling of the original words or to make the meaning of the quotes clearer. All metric conversions in this book are approximate.*

CHAPTER ONE

Roger Williams and the Puritans

WHAT

Roger Williams is forced out of Massachusetts over
political and religious differences with the colony's leaders.

ISSUE

Separation of church and state

WHERE

Massachusetts

WHEN

1635

*S*tarting in 1620, English Protestants known as Separatists began to settle in Plymouth, Massachusetts. (Today, they are known as Pilgrims.) Almost a decade later, Puritans reached the Boston area, about 40 miles (64 kilometers) northwest of Plymouth. The Puritans and Separatists shared many beliefs based on the teachings of Swiss religious thinker John Calvin. These "Calvinists" believed that God chose people at birth to go to Heaven after they died. Living a good life was no guarantee of going to Heaven, yet believers were expected to live as if they were chosen, and that meant following all the teachings in the Bible.

> *Fast Fact*
>
> Within their theocracy, the Calvinists had some democratic practices. Civil leaders were elected, though only members of the church could vote.

The Separatists and Puritans had come to America so that they could freely practice their religion. In England, the government limited the religious practices of people who did not belong to the official Church of England. The English monarch was the head of the church, and following church teachings was a political issue, as well as a religious one. When the Calvinists reached Massachusetts, they created a political system based on their beliefs. Their goal was a theocracy—a government controlled by religious leaders and their understanding of the Bible. The Calvinists also believed that a civil society was formed by people freely coming together and agreeing to live by certain rules—God's rules. What brought the Massachusetts Separatists and Puritans together was their belief in God, Jesus Christ, and the authority of the Bible.

The Arrival of Roger Williams

In 1631, a minister named Roger Williams arrived in Massachusetts. He was offered a job in Boston, where the Puritans still accepted the idea of remaining in the English national church, but Williams was a Separatist. He went to the nearby town of Salem, where he hoped that he could follow his Separatist beliefs. Salem, however, was heavily influenced by the leaders in Boston, who convinced Salem officials that Williams was not a proper minister because of his beliefs. After first offering Williams a job, the Salem congregation changed its mind. Williams moved on again, heading for the Separatist colony of Plymouth.

By the end of 1633, Williams was having disagreements with the leaders in Plymouth, and he returned to Salem. Wherever he went, pursuing his own strict brand of Calvinism, Williams could not seem to avoid arguments. Williams also created enemies with his ideas on politics. He claimed that the English king, Charles I, did not have a legal right to grant land to the Massachusetts settlers. The land belonged to the Native Americans of the region; it was not Charles's to give away.

Over the next two years, Williams continued to speak out on a number of issues. In March 1635, he appeared before the General Court, the government of Massachusetts Bay, because the leaders of the colony were opposed to his religious and political beliefs. The General Court considered taking action against him but let him go. In July, he appeared before the court again. The court said that Williams's ideas were "very dangerous."

> *Fast Fact*
>
> Salem was the first town settled by the English Puritans, who had received permission from the English king, Charles I, to form a colony in North America. The colony was called Massachusetts Bay. Boston, however, soon became the colony's major town.

UNDERSTANDING THE NAMES

The Puritans wanted to purify, or reform, the national church in England so that it followed their beliefs. The Separatists wanted to separate completely from the national church. The Massachusetts Puritans were also known as Congregationalists. They thought that each local church, or congregation, should choose its own minister and run its own affairs.

A New Colony

In October 1635, the General Court banished Williams. By this time, the leaders in Plymouth did not want him back either. By January, he had not left, and Massachusetts officials were ready to force him to return to England. Instead, Williams and a few supporters slipped out of the colony. They reached what is now Rhode Island and bought land from the local natives. Williams founded a town and named it Providence.

Within three years, about thirty families lived in Providence. Williams indicated that people with any religious beliefs were welcome there. In 1637, another Puritan, Anne Hutchinson, joined this new community. Hutchinson had preached several ideas that went against Puritan teachings, and the General Court forced her out of Massachusetts. She stopped in Providence before setting up a new community in Portsmouth. This town, along with Providence, Newport, and Warwick, formed the heart of the Rhode Island colony.

Famous Figures

ANNE HUTCHINSON
(1591–1643)

Anne Hutchinson came to Massachusetts in 1634. At first, she loyally accepted Puritan teachings, but by 1636, she was following a different path. She strongly supported the idea that doing good deeds would not guarantee a person's place in Heaven—but Hutchinson went even further, saying that those who were chosen by God did not have to follow all laws and moral teachings, as Puritans believed they should. Hutchinson also claimed that God made direct contact with his chosen people while they were still on Earth, an idea that Puritan leaders rejected. Hutchinson was brought to trial in 1637 for spreading false beliefs. After her stay in Rhode Island, Hutchinson settled on Long Island, where she was killed during a Native American raid.

Anne Hutchinson's opinions about religion angered the Puritan leaders in the Massachusetts colony. The fact that Hutchinson was a woman made her ideas even more threatening, since at that time women were rarely so outspoken. Hutchinson was murdered during a Native American raid on Long Island, New York, in 1643.

In Providence, Williams and his followers started the first Baptist church in America. Both Puritans and Separatists looked down on the Baptists, who believed that people should be baptized only as adults, after finding God on their own. (Other Christian groups baptized babies.) Williams also had political concerns. In 1644, he sailed to England to get a charter for his colony. The charter ensured that neighboring colonies could not claim Rhode Island's land as their own. He also continued to debate his Puritan critics, writing a book that presented his ideas on religion and politics.

Williams's Argument

Williams, like other Calvinists, thought that only faith in God allowed people to restrain their bad side and do good. Like the Massachusetts Puritans, Williams wanted the church to be as pure and good as possible. The best way to do this, he believed, was to keep the church out of human concerns—such as politics. The church and its leaders should focus on God and His teachings. The Puritans and Pilgrims of Massachusetts rejected this idea of separating church and state, setting up the disagreement between them and Williams.

During 1634 and 1635, several issues pitted Williams against the leaders of Massachusetts Bay. For example, Williams opposed forcing nonbelievers to take a loyalty oath. All men over sixteen were supposed to swear their loyalty to the government. The oath ended with the words "so help me God." Williams did not think a nonbeliever should be promising to do something in God's name. He thought that the oath was an insult to God.

Unlike the Puritans, Williams saw that non-Christians could be good citizens. They could follow civil laws while still practicing their own beliefs. Williams opposed governing by Puritan teachings, which might deny the rights of these nonbelievers. He also believed that just because a government official was a Puritan, it did not mean that he would always rule fairly or well.

> *Fast Fact*
>
> Williams's good relations with Native Americans helped him and his followers survive in their new home. Both Wampanoag and Narragansett tribes gave the settlers food and seeds so they could plant their own crops.

Williams admitted that there could be some doubt about the best way to worship God. To him, that was another reason to let members of other faiths worship as they chose. Since the Puritans could not be sure that their ideas of worship were right, they should not create a state that limited free worship. In Rhode Island, Williams allowed the practice of many different religions.

Famous Figures

ROGER WILLIAMS
(1603–1683)

One Puritan leader called Roger Williams "divinely mad." No one questioned Williams's devotion to his faith, but his ideas struck some Puritans as slightly crazy. Even harder for them to accept was Williams's absolute belief that his ideas were right and everyone else's were wrong.

Born in London, England, Williams studied to become a minister while still in England. In America, he founded the colony of Rhode Island after being forced to leave Massachusetts. Williams served as governor of Rhode Island from 1654 to 1657.

The Puritan Arguments against Williams

To survive in North America, the Puritans believed that they needed to strictly enforce religious and civil laws. Their leaders expected all citizens to accept these laws. Almost as soon as Williams arrived in America, however, he was a threat. He questioned basic Puritan ideas. His "strange opinions," as Plymouth leader William Bradford put it, led to the conflict between Williams and the Puritans. To Williams, however, his approach was the only correct way to worship God.

In religious issues, Puritan leader John Cotton headed the defense of the Puritan approach. He argued that the Bible supported the Puritan view of combining the state and the church. He believed that both civil and religious powers came through Christ and that civil rulers should carry out his teachings. In 1636, Cotton wrote, "None are so fit to be trusted with the liberties of the [state] as church members." Cotton also argued against Williams's Separatist beliefs. Cotton said that the Puritans had taken a middle path between rejecting the Church of England altogether and following its mistaken policies.

Fast Fact

Congregationalism remained the official religion in Massachusetts until 1833.

For many years, Cotton and Williams wrote long documents attacking each other's ideas and promoting their own. Each man had complete faith that his ideas were correct. At times, the exchanges became personal. Cotton wrote that Williams considered him a man of "meaner note." In return, Cotton thought Williams was arrogant, as he seemed to believe that it was "his duty to give public advertisement...of the corruptions of religion which [he] observe[s] in [others'] judgment and practice."

With his founding of Rhode Island, Williams was able to put his ideas on the separation of church and state into practice. However, in Massachusetts and other Puritan areas of New England, the combining of civil and religious power lasted for many decades. Then, during the eighteenth century, more Americans began to call for the separation of church and state. That notion is now part of the U.S. Constitution. Still, many Americans continue to debate the role—if any—that religion should play in government.

In Their Own Words

Here is part of *The Examiner—Defended in a Fair and Sober Answer,* one of Roger Williams's works.

Christ's interest in this [state], or any, is the freedom of the souls of his people. I confess that all nations, all people, kings, princes, judges...ought to kiss the Son, be nursing fathers and mothers to Christ Jesus and his followers; but what a dreadful mistake is this, that no people must live but Christians?

Famous Figures

JOHN COTTON

(1584–1652)

A respected Puritan minister in England, John Cotton played a large role in developing Congregational Puritanism in America. He believed that in Massachusetts, only church members should govern civil society. He also wanted the government to closely follow the laws set down by Moses in the Bible. Cotton was the grandfather of Cotton Mather, a Boston minister who played an important role in the Salem witch trials of 1692.

In Their Own Words

In 1647, Puritan minister Nathaniel Ward attacked Williams and others who wanted religious freedom. Here's part of what he wrote.

I...proclaim to the world, in the name of our colony, that all [non-Puritans] shall have free liberty to keep away from us, and such as will come to be gone as fast as they can, the sooner the better.... I...[say] that God does nowhere in His Word tolerate Christian states to give tolerations to such [enemies] of His truth, if they have power in their hands to suppress them.

CHAPTER TWO

King Philip's War

WHAT
Native American tribes battle New England colonists.

ISSUE
Control of traditional Native American lands

WHERE
Massachusetts, Rhode Island, and Connecticut

WHEN
1675–1676

*I*n 1620, English settlers now known as Pilgrims landed in Plymouth, Massachusetts. They had left Europe so that they could freely practice their religion. The Pilgrims' brand of Protestant faith was different from the official religion of England, and the Pilgrims could not worship as they chose at home. In America, they believed, they could build a new society based on their religious beliefs.

However, the settlers faced problems in their new home. They landed as winter approached, and disease and a lack of food killed about half of them. Help came in the spring of 1621, when a Wampanoag native named Tisquantum arrived at Plymouth. Years before, he had been kidnapped by an English trader and taken to Europe. Speaking English, the helpful native served as a translator between the settlers and Usamequin, the sachem, or leader, of the Wampanoag. Usamequin was known to the English as Massasoit, which means "great chief."

The English and the Wampanoag signed a peace treaty. The English, outnumbered and facing starvation, needed native help to survive. To Massasoit, the English represented a potential ally in any future wars with the Narragansett, the traditional enemy of the Wampanoag. In addition to not attacking each other, the two sides agreed that "if any did unjustly war against [Massasoit], they [the English] would aid him; if any did war against them, he should aid them."

With Tisquantum's help, the English learned Native American farming methods that enabled them to survive in their new home. That fall, the English invited the Wampanoag to celebrate the harvest. This feast is considered the first Thanksgiving, and the good relations enjoyed by the two sides endured for many years.

PILGRIMS AND PURITANS

The religious settlers at Plymouth called themselves Saints. Others called them Separatists, because they wanted to separate from the official Church of England. The settlers also included some English people who did not share Separatist beliefs. They were known as Strangers. In religious attitudes, the Separatists were close to the Puritans, who first arrived in the Boston, Massachusetts, area in 1628. The Puritan colony, called Massachusetts Bay, became larger and more powerful than the Pilgrim colony in Plymouth. In 1691, Plymouth became part of Massachusetts.

The Rise of Metacomet

Massasoit had two sons, Wamsutta and Metacomet. The English called them Alexander and Philip. Wamsutta, the older of the two brothers, became sachem after Massasoit's death. The English asked him to come to Plymouth to explain his recent sale of lands to colonists in Rhode Island. The sachem did not come, so the Pilgrim leaders sent armed men to bring Wamsutta by force. After being questioned, Wamsutta fell ill and died on the trip home. Some Wampanoag believed that the English had poisoned their leader. This suspicion led to a growing distrust and hatred of the English. With his brother's death, Metacomet became sachem. He was sometimes known as King Philip.

Life for the Wampanoag had grown harder while Massasoit was still alive. Diseases brought over from Europe killed thousands of Native Americans across southern New England. In the meantime, more English settlers came to the region, eager to acquire Wampanoag land. Massasoit traded the land for goods in deals that usually favored the English. The colonists began living closer to the natives and expecting them to follow the colonies' laws. The English also tried to convert the Wampanoag to

Christianity. Some natives did not like to see their traditional religious beliefs and practices replaced by the Pilgrims' religion.

Metacomet saw all the changes that had come as the English continued to arrive in New England. The sachem realized that his people would have to fight the English to preserve their land and culture. He began recruiting other tribes to aid him in resisting the English. Most, however, wanted good relations with the colonists and were not eager to join Metacomet's cause.

Massasoit (center) was the leader of the Wampanoag at the time of the first English settlement in Massachusetts. After he and the leaders of the English colony signed a treaty, the Native Americans taught the settlers farming techniques and helped them survive in the new land. At the end of the first successful harvest, the colonists and Native Americans had a feast, considered the first Thanksgiving.

War across New England

In January 1675, a Praying Indian named Sassamon was found dead under the ice of a frozen lake. English authorities immediately assumed that Metacomet was somehow responsible. Three Wampanoag close to the sachem were accused of the crime, found guilty, and executed. Metacomet said that the murder—if it was truly a murder—was a Wampanoag affair that should have been decided by the tribal justice system, not an English court. The incident fueled Metacomet's anger and called for war.

That June, a group of Wampanoag entered the town of Swansea, Massachusetts. They raided local farms, killing animals and looking for things to steal. On June 24, a boy shot and killed one of these Wampanoag raiders. In response, the natives killed several residents of the town.

Famous Figures

METACOMET
(c.1642–1676)

The second son of Massasoit, Metacomet was raised to be a warrior and a leader. As a young man, he visited Boston and impressed residents with his fine clothes and wampum belts, which were long strings of seashells. Wampum was prized by the Native Americans as jewelry and a form of money, and for many years, the English used it as money, too. However, Plymouth leaders viewed Metacomet with suspicion once he became sachem. Three times, they brought him to trial for plotting against the English. As late as 1671, Metacomet pledged his loyalty to the English, yet he was also increasingly angry with the colonists' treatment of him and his people. Once King Philip's War (1675–1676) began, Metacomet led an alliance of native tribes against the English.

By this time, Metacomet had been able to find other tribes willing to fight the English. These included the Nipmucks and Pocassets. Later, the Wampanoag's former foes, the Narragansett, also joined Metacomet's side. For several months, the Wampanoag and their allies attacked towns and villages across southern New England. The fighting also spread to southern Maine, which at that time was part of Massachusetts.

In the spring of 1676, Metacomet led attacks on several towns, including Plymouth. In July, the natives and English fought near Monthaup. The English captured Metacomet's wife and son and sold them into slavery. Hearing the news, the sachem said, "My heart breaks. Now I am ready to die." A few weeks later, the English found Metacomet's camp and killed him. Some natives loyal to Metacomet continued to fight, but the English had won King Philip's War.

Most Wampanoag who survived the war were sold into slavery. Many of their allies moved north or west. In all, about 9,000 people died during the war—two-thirds of them Native Americans. Metacomet was the last Native American of the region to lead a war against the English. His people would never regain their old ways.

Over time, several tribes formed alliances with the Wampanoag, including their traditional enemies the Narragansett to fight the settlers.

Metacomet's Complaints

To Metacomet and other natives of the region, their war against the English was just. The Wampanoag and the other tribes of New England viewed property and land much differently than the settlers did. To the natives, individuals (or even tribes) did not own land. Land was provided by nature for everyone to use. The land that the Wampanoag used was theirs by tradition, not because they had purchased it.

The arrival of the English changed the Native Americans' relation to the land. When Massasoit or another sachem signed a deal with the settlers, the English thought that they were buying land that became theirs until they chose to sell it to someone else. The natives, however, typically thought that they were merely agreeing to let the settlers use the land.

Over time, these differing views on land owner-ship and use created problems. Sometimes the English built fences to keep their farm animals on "their" prop-erty. The natives saw the fences as obstacles to their traditional hunting grounds, which they believed they still had a right to use.

When the settlers did not build fences, their animals roamed onto lands where the natives hunted and farmed. In response to this animal "invasion," some Native Americans killed cows or hogs that strayed off their owners' land. The natives saw this as protecting their own food supply. The English treated the killings as theft of their property and brought the natives to court for breaking English laws—laws that the natives did not necessarily recognize.

By 1660, the Wampanoag also faced new economic pressures. When the English first arrived, they had traded with the Native Americans of New England for beaver furs and wampum. Over time,

Fast Fact

Puritan and Pilgrim laws were based on the Bible and religious beliefs. Sunday was a day devoted to going to church—and nothing else. Wampanoag and other Native Americans were arrested and fined for such activi-ties as traveling, transporting apples, and firing guns on Sunday.

however, European coins began to replace wampum as money, and beaver fur lost popularity in Europe, thus limiting the Wampanoag's ability to trade for tools and other goods.

On the one hand, the Wampanoag were losing their land to the settlers, so they could not hunt and farm as they once had. On the other, they lacked items that the English wanted to buy. Many native men were forced to work for low wages on English farms. In Wampanoag society, farming was a woman's job. Doing farm work for the colonists was an insult. To Metacomet and others, war seemed the only solution for preserving Wampanoag land and pride.

In Their Own Words

Before the start of King Philip's War, Metacomet spoke of his feelings about the English. Here is some of what he said, as recorded by John Easton, a colonial leader from Rhode Island.

When the English first came, [Metacomet's] father was a great man, and…he constrained other Indians from wronging the English, and gave them corn and showed them how to plant. But [Metacomet's] brother, when he was king, came miserably to die, by being forced to court, as they judged poisoned. And another grievance was, if twenty of their honest Indians testified that an Englishman had done them wrong, it was nothing; and if but one of their worst Indians testified against any Indian or their king, when it pleased the English, it was sufficient….

The English View on Natives and Their Land

The Pilgrims' and the Puritans' view of life in New England was drastically different from Metacomet's. These two groups believed that God had chosen them to come to North America and create a new society based on the teachings of the Bible. To the Pilgrims, their new home was filled with "wild beasts and wild men," as one Plymouth governor put it. The settlers' goal was to tame both the land and the wild natives who lived there.

The Pilgrims wanted to control the land by clearing trees and building fences. One Puritan leader explained that since the Native Americans did not fence in land and build towns, the English had a God-given right to take what they needed and leave the Native Americans the rest.

Some Pilgrims and Puritans insulted the natives, calling them lazy and savage. Roger Williams, the founder of Rhode Island, noted that Narragansett sachems were threatened with war if they did not become Christians.

Williams disapproved of the typical Puritan attitude toward the Algonquians. Most colonial leaders, however, shaped their political and religious policies without considering the natives' interests. The colonists did not see how their actions might upset the Wampanoag or harm their way of life. When war came in 1675, the settlers believed that God was on their side. In Boston, they asked for God's help in "subduing the heathen and returning [the soldiers] in safety to their families." Many Americans held a negative attitude toward Native Americans into the twentieth century.

Fast Fact

Another settler who looked for peaceful solutions to problems with the Native Americans was John Easton of Rhode Island. He invited Metacomet to a peace conference in 1675 and tried to create a council with English and Native American members to address Wampanoag concerns. The council never met.

In Their Own Words

Cotton Mather, a minister from Boston, recorded the events of one battle of King Philip's War. His description shows the settlers' attitudes toward the Native Americans.

We have heard of two and twenty Indian captains slain, all of them brought down to Hell in one day. When they came to see the ashes of their friends...and the bodies...terribly barbecued, where the English had been doing a good day's work, they...were the pictures of...desperation.

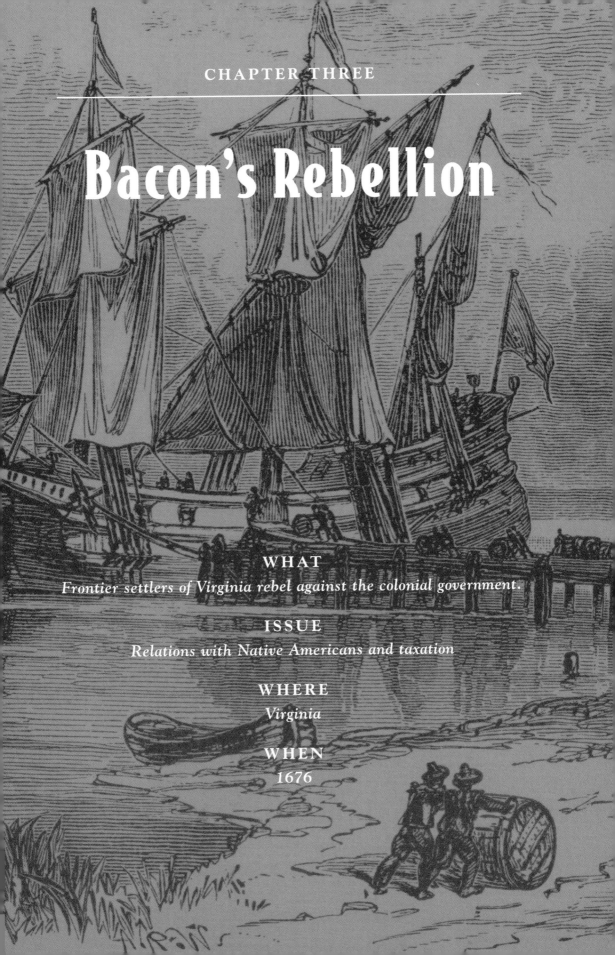

CHAPTER THREE

Bacon's Rebellion

WHAT
Frontier settlers of Virginia rebel against the colonial government.

ISSUE
Relations with Native Americans and taxation

WHERE
Virginia

WHEN
1676

*D*uring the 1670s, Virginia politics and society were dominated by the colony's wealthy tobacco planters. These farmers owned large plantations along Chesapeake Bay and major rivers. Supporting their interests was Governor William Berkeley. He gave his friends important positions in the government, and they—along with Berkeley—dominated the fur trade with the colony's Native Americans.

New arrivals to Virginia or farmers without much money had to head toward the Virginia frontier to buy land. Many Virginians could not afford to buy land at all, so they rented farmland from the wealthy. The colony's tax policies hit renters and poorer landowners the worst. They paid a tax on themselves, their sons over sixteen, and any servants and slaves. Meanwhile, planters who served in the government did not pay the tax.

Trade and farm policies added to the frontier farmers' difficulties. The cost of shipping tobacco overseas had risen because of English laws that required the colonies to ship all their goods on English vessels. Virginia farmers were also facing competition from tobacco grown in Maryland and North Carolina. With more tobacco being sold, the prices for it fell. In 1676, a severe drought added to the Virginians' concerns.

Frontier farmers also faced the threat of attack by Native Americans. In general, the Virginians had good relations with the tribes that had been in the area when the English first arrived. Starting in the 1660s, however, Susquehannock natives had moved into the region from Pennsylvania. They took part in several battles and raids against the colonists. Relations with Native Americans on the frontier worsened in 1675, after settlers and natives fought several minor skirmishes.

Fast Fact

One of the Virginia officers who led an attack on frontier tribes was Colonel John Washington, grandfather of George Washington.

SIR WILLIAM BERKELEY

(1606–1677)

By some historical accounts, William Berkeley was a popular governor in Virginia. Others, however, say that he ruled largely to benefit himself and his wealthy friends. Berkeley was a loyal supporter of King Charles I and was made a knight in 1639. Two years later, Berkeley was named governor of Virginia. He held that position for most of the next thirty-five years. Berkeley opposed a free press and free schools, saying that they encouraged disobedience to government and the church. He also did not call for elections in the assembly, Virginia's lawmaking body, for fifteen years, from 1661 to 1676. During that time, the assembly passed many laws that favored the rich in the colony. Berkeley died in England after Bacon's Rebellion.

Starting a Rebellion

One of the frontier farmers was Nathaniel Bacon. In the spring of 1676, he took command of a group of volunteer soldiers who wanted to defend the frontier. That March, Virginia's lawmakers had declared war against the Native Americans but had distinguished between friendly tribes and the Susquehannock. Bacon, however, wanted to attack them all. The March declaration of war had also called for more taxes to pay for military costs. Many frontier farmers did not want to pay another tax that they could not afford.

Bacon and his troops raided lands owned by friendly natives. Berkeley demanded that Bacon end his military actions and let the regular militia lead the volunteers, since that was its job. Bacon, however, stayed in command. By this time, he was gaining support from renters, servants, slaves, and others who opposed all of Berkeley's policies.

In May, Berkeley demanded that Bacon turn himself in to stand trial as a rebel. The governor also called for an election to choose a new assembly. At that time in Virginia, only landowners were allowed to vote, but for that election, the governor let all free men vote. Thanks to that change, many of Bacon's supporters were elected to the assembly. Bacon himself won a seat, though he was reluctant to go to the capital of Jamestown, since Berkeley still wanted to arrest him.

In June, Bacon finally came to Jamestown. He asked Berkeley to forgive him, and the governor did, dropping the charges against him. Berkeley then promised that Bacon would receive an officer's rank in the militia and be allowed to raise a force to fight the Native Americans. The two men argued, however, over how much power Bacon would have. Bacon demanded to be named "general of all the forces in Virginia against the Indians." He backed up his demand with armed men. Faced with that threat, Berkeley agreed. Bacon and his supporters then asked for changes in the colony's laws, including requiring government officials to pay taxes and making it easier for debtors to pay the money that they owed. In late June, the assembly passed these laws.

A Colonial Civil War

Bacon left Jamestown to lead the fight against the Native Americans. Soon Bacon's men were reported to be taking weapons and horses away from people loyal to Berkeley. Berkeley saw that Bacon was abusing his power—which he had gained through threat of violence—and decided once again that the new general was a rebel. When Bacon learned that Berkeley was organizing troops to stop him, he began arresting the governor's supporters and taking their lands. By now, more of the common people were supporting Bacon and his rebellion. Berkeley fled to Virginia's Eastern Shore, a rural region on the east side of Chesapeake Bay. A few other wealthy landowners soon joined him there.

In early August, Bacon and his supporters began forming a new government for Virginia. At a political convention, Bacon was named the leader of the colony, and citizens were required to swear their loyalty to the new government.

From the Eastern Shore, Berkeley organized a force to try to end the rebellion. In September, loyalist troops captured a rebel ship and then took control of Jamestown. The rebels, however, attacked the capital and defeated a much larger loyalist force. Bacon's army then torched the city, starting a fire that destroyed many homes and public buildings.

Fast Fact

A group of women nicknamed "news wives" spoke out against Berkeley and rallied support for Bacon.

Famous Figures

NATHANIEL BACON
(1647–1676)

Nathaniel Bacon was the son of a wealthy Englishman. In 1674, Bacon's father sent him and his wife to Virginia. Using his father's money, Bacon bought a plantation. William Berkeley was a cousin of Bacon's, and the governor named the young man to a government council. Bacon, however, did not show much interest in politics until he challenged Berkeley's power in 1676. Bacon led a small group of educated, wealthy farmers who were not tied to Berkeley and his supporters. Later, Bacon won the support of common Virginians who opposed the governor.

Bacon and his followers burned Jamestown in September 1676.

The End of the Rebellion

At the end of September, two ships arrived from England. Their captains helped Berkeley's forces gain control of Virginia's waterways. In late October, Bacon died, probably from a stomach ailment called dysentery. The rebellion continued, but Berkeley gained more allies and began to win victories on the battlefield. In December, Thomas Grantham, the captain of another ship helping Berkeley, told the rebels that the king was going to study the rebels' complaints against the colonial government and make reforms. Most of Bacon's men then decided to end the rebellion.

Now back in power, Berkeley began a series of trials. The governor pardoned some rebels, but a number of the leaders were found guilty of treason and executed. At this time, the end of January 1677, a fleet of ships arrived from England. They carried 1,000 troops and three commissioners, representatives of

Charles II. The commissioners' job was to find out how the rebellion had started.

The commissioners asked the residents to list their complaints about the government. They also told the Virginians that the king had pardoned all the rebels. Ignoring this fact, Berkeley continued to try them for treason. The commissioners then recommended that Berkeley be removed as governor. As they wrote, "We think it impossible...that ever things should be put into that peaceable posture and happy composure desired...while Sir William continues [as governor]."

Fast Fact

Captain Grantham promised the servants and slaves who had fought the loyalists that they would keep their freedom if they stopped fighting. Berkeley, however, broke that promise and sent them back to their masters.

Bacon's Arguments against the Government

Some Virginians had complained about Berkeley and his policies before 1676. However, the March declaration of war against the natives brought an especially bitter response. Bacon was just one of the frontier planters who believed that his life was in danger because of the native attacks. A worker on his plantation had already been killed in one raid.

Bacon and his supporters thought that Berkeley was not doing enough to fight the natives. A tax, passed in 1675, was collected to build forts on the frontier, but the frontier farmers complained that the forts the government built "were made of mud and dirt and so of no use." The governor chose his friends to build and command the forts. They kept some of the tax money for themselves instead of spending it on the forts. At first, Bacon and the other rebels focused on the military issue of fighting the Native Americans. The tax issue, however, was always a concern to the rebels.

Fast Fact

At one point in the battle at Jamestown, the rebels used the wives of loyalists as shields so that the loyalist troops would not fire on them.

In July 1676, Bacon expanded his public complaints against the governor. He issued a document called "Declaration in the Name of the People." Bacon asserted that Berkeley had given his friends important government jobs, raised taxes too high, and controlled the beaver trade with the natives. Berkeley, Bacon said, was a traitor to King Charles II for these actions.

The royal commission that studied Bacon's Rebellion also criticized the governor's actions. It said that in January 1676, Berkeley had called back a military force that was prepared to hunt for Susquehannock natives. This step left "the poor inhabitants under continual and deadly fears and terrors of their lives." The commission faulted the governor for the trials and executions conducted after the war. The king's representatives also accepted many of the complaints against the high taxes and the influence that Berkeley's friends had on the government.

In Their Own Words

In his "Declaration in the Name of the People," Nathaniel Bacon gave a list of charges against William Berkeley. They included

...[Raising] great unjust taxes upon the commonality for the advancement of private favorites and other sinister ends...

...[Having] protected, favored, and emboldened the Indians against his Majesty's loyal subjects, never...requiring or appointing any due or proper means of satisfaction for their many invasions, robberies, and murders committed upon us.

...[Raising] and effecting civil war and destruction...

Berkeley Defends Himself

In 1675, Berkeley was convinced that his policy toward the natives was the right one. He wanted to stay on friendly terms with the Algonquian natives who had accepted English rule. Berkeley refused to believe Bacon's argument that all Native Americans posed a threat to the settlers. He also knew that settlers sometimes disrupted the natives' lifestyle. A government report written after the rebellion described how frontier settlers' animals "[destroyed] all the corn of the other Indians of the town." According to this report, the settlers who had "intruded" sparked the war with the natives.

The royal commission, though it faulted some of Berkeley's actions, did seem to support his Native American policy. In their report, the commissioners attacked the "inconsiderate sort of men" who "so rashly...call up war, and seem to wish and aim at an utter [destruction] of the Indians (and are yet still the first that complain and murmur at the charge and taxes that...attends such a war)."

Once the rebellion ended, Berkeley traveled to England to face Charles II in the spring of 1677. The king was angry that Berkeley had not come earlier, as he had been ordered. Berkeley did not live long enough to defend himself, dying in July. His friends and relatives argued his case with the government. They noted that "there is not one private [complaint] brought against Sir William Berkeley before the rebellion."

Despite Berkeley's defense of his actions, Charles II and his advisers seemed to blame the governor for the rebellion. The new governor, Colonel Herbert Jeffreys, named some of Bacon's supporters to help him run the colony. English troops remained in Virginia for several years. By the 1690s, the government in Virginia had lowered taxes. Rising tobacco prices also helped ease some of the complaints about government

Fast Fact

One charge against Berkeley was that he let his friends sell ammunition to the Native Americans, even though this was forbidden after March 1676. The royal commission that studied the rebellion did not find any evidence to support this claim.

policies. Bacon's supporters gained backing for their desire to fight the Native Americans when necessary to protect planters settling along the frontier.

In Their Own Words

In May 1676, Berkeley defended himself and criticized Nathaniel Bacon for leading an attack on Native Americans in Virginia. Here is part of what he wrote.

...I do not know of any thing relative to this country wherein I have acted unjustly, corruptly, or negligently in distributing equal justice to all men, and taking all possible care to defend their properties....

...[That] very action which [Bacon] boasts of was sickly and foolishly...and treacherously carried to the dishonor of the English nation...and I doubt not but by God's assistance to have better success than Bacon hath had, the reasons of my hopes are, that I will take council of wiser men than myself, but Bacon hath none about him.

CHAPTER FOUR

The Salem Witch Trials

WHAT
Young girls accuse more than 150 people of being witches.

ISSUE
The usefulness and legality of the trials

WHERE
Salem, Massachusetts

WHEN
1692–1693

*T*he Puritans who settled most of New England brought a strong, strict faith to their new home. They believed that God chose certain people to go to Heaven, and nothing that humans did on Earth could change their fate after they died. Yet the Puritans insisted that people should behave as if they were chosen. They should go to church, follow the Ten Commandments, and read the Bible. The Puritans' faith influenced every part of daily life, including the legal system. A person might be whipped for missing Sunday church, and a married couple could be punished for kissing in public.

To the Puritans, the devil, or Satan, was just as real as God. The devil tempted Christians to do evil deeds and made deals with people seeking his aid. Christians of many faiths believed that certain people chose to become witches, promising to serve the devil. In return, the devil gave them the power to cast harmful spells on others. People found guilty of being witches were executed.

Women were considered most likely to fall under the devil's influence. In 1608, a Puritan minister wrote, "The woman, being the weaker sex, is soon entangled by the devil's illusions." Though women were considered "weak," the courts could not go easy on a woman found guilty of being a witch: "[Though] it be a woman and the weaker vessel, she shall not escape...she must die the death."

The English had many tales about witchcraft and other events that could not be explained by reason. These supernatural happenings included predicting the future. People also used certain good luck charms that they thought would keep away evil. Some Christians took part in these practices. A few believers thought they had a gift that came from God, and they were sometimes known as "healing witches." "True" witches, however, were clearly tied to Satan and tried to harm people they did not like.

Fast Fact

A 1641 Massachusetts law ordered the death penalty for anyone found guilty of practicing witchcraft. Connecticut had a similar law. Around 1647, one of the first executions of a witch in New England took place in that colony.

Troubles in Salem

In January 1692, Samuel Parris was the minister in Salem Village, a part of the larger town of Salem, Massachusetts. In one of his first sermons for the new year, Parris talked about the devil. "It is the main drift of the devil," he said, "to pull [the church] down." He mentioned that "wicked" people served as the "assistants of Satan" in this effort.

Parris and his wife, Elizabeth, had three children. A niece, Abigail, also lived with them, and the household included two Native American slaves, Tituba and John. Sometime around the beginning of 1692, Abigail and her eight-year-old cousin, Betty, began using some of the traditional English methods for trying to predict the future. A few other neighborhood girls sometimes joined them.

By the middle of January, Betty and Abigail were acting strangely. They often made weird motions or spoke gibberish, and at times, they complained of pains. Their behavior continued for weeks, and some people suggested that the girls were under a witch's spell. The first person suspected of being a witch was Tituba. She admitted that a former master had been a witch and taught her how to detect witchcraft, but the slave insisted that she was not a witch.

By late February, the two other girls who had played the supernatural games with Betty and Abigail also seemed to be bedeviled, or under the devil's influence. One girl, Ann Putnam, said she saw the specter, or ghostly image, of Sarah Good, a local woman. Ann said that the specter tried to make her sign a book. A common belief of the time was that Satan made witches sign their names in a book, creating a contract between him and those seeking his aid. The other girl, Elizabeth Hubbard, claimed that another local woman, Sarah Osborn, had appeared to her in spectral form.

Famous Figures

TITUBA

Many of the stories once told about Tituba are not true. They were made up by New Englanders after the Salem witch trials. She was most likely a Native American from South America who was sold into slavery in the Caribbean. She and her future husband, John, might have come with Samuel Parris from Barbados when he settled in Massachusetts in 1680. It is possible, however, that Parris bought them in Massachusetts. In Salem Village, Tituba took care of the Parris children. She was later accused of having taught magic and fortune-telling to the young girls, who accused others of witchcraft. Today, most historians doubt this, since the Venus glass used by the girls was an English tradition. According to one account from the late seventeenth century, Tituba claimed that Parris beat her to force her to confess to being a witch. Because Tituba confessed, she was not executed, but she did spend more than a year in jail.

Fast Fact

One tool that the Salem girls used to predict the future was a "Venus glass." They dropped an egg white into a glass of water. The egg formed patterns that supposedly suggested what would happen in the future.

The Trials Begin

The girls' bizarre behavior continued, and the local officials arrested Tituba, Good, and Osborn, charging them with practicing witchcraft. A crowd filled the local meetinghouse where the officials examined the accused. Questioned first, Good denied that she was a witch or had tormented the four young girls. The girls were asked if Good was the person who had hurt them. As the record reports, "So they did all look upon her and said this was one of the persons that did torment them." At the same time, the girls had violent fits, twisting their bodies into painful positions and falling to the floor.

During the questioning, Good accused Osborn of being the girls' tormentor. Osborn, an elderly woman in poor health, denied the charge of witchcraft. The girls, however, insisted that she was a witch and that she had appeared to them in spectral form. When Tituba was questioned, she said that she saw four specters hurt the children. Then the slave shocked the crowd by admitting that she had been visited by a man in spectral form. She told them, "He said he would kill the children, and...if I would not serve him he would do so to me." Tituba said Osborn and Good were witches, as well.

The three women were placed in jail to await their trial. In the weeks that followed, Ann Putnam claimed she saw the specters of the women and also saw other people in spectral form. The three other girls usually backed up her claims with reports of their own visions. New accusers also stepped forward, describing specters that came to them and did them harm.

By the end of April 1692, more than two dozen people were in jail, accused of being witches. They included several men. One of them, John Proctor, was a successful farmer and tavern keeper in Salem Village. He had questioned whether the first people arrested and tried for witchcraft were actually witches. To those who supported the "witch hunt," this doubt was another sign that he was a witch.

In June, Massachusetts governor Sir William Phips called for the first trial of the accused witches. Bridget Bishop was the first person found guilty and executed for being a witch. By the end of September, eighteen more people were hanged, including Proctor and Good. Osborn died in jail. Another accused witch, Giles Corey, was pressed to death under rocks. He had refused to stand trial for his alleged crime. The rocks were meant to torture him until he spoke, but their weight killed him first.

Fast Fact

As the hunt for witches spread, the Salem jail could not hold all of the accused. Many of them were jailed in Boston, the capital of Massachusetts.

Nearly twenty convicted witches had been executed as a result of the witchcraft trials. Governor Phips managed to have the trials stopped by October 1692.

The End of the Trials

After the September hangings, Salem residents continued to accuse others of witchcraft. By this time, however, some important people were thinking that the trials and executions had gone too far. More than 100 people had been accused of being witches, including Mary Phips, wife of the Massachusetts governor. In October, Governor Phips ordered the trials to stop. As Phips wrote to the English government, he was concerned that some "innocent subjects" were in danger of being falsely convicted and executed.

In January 1693, a second court began hearing trials for the fifty or so people still in jail for alleged witchcraft. This time, jurors were not allowed to consider an accuser's claim of spectral torment in deciding if someone was a witch. The trials ended with just three people found guilty. Phips later used his powers as governor to free them and five others who had already been convicted.

PUTNAM'S CONFESSION

Most historians consider Ann Putnam to be the leader of the girls who accused others of being witches. She named more than sixty people as tormentors. In 1706, while still living in Salem, she gave a statement about her role in the witch trials. She apologized for her actions and said, "Now I have just grounds and good reason to believe they were innocent persons; and that it was a great delusion of Satan that deceived me in that sad time."

Supporters of the Witch Trials

Given the nature of Puritan beliefs, many people were ready to accept the idea that witches were harming the residents of Salem. Deodat Lawson, a minister, attended many of the early hearings. Watching the girls shake and twist their bodies, he was convinced that the fits were "much beyond the ordinary force of the same persons when they were in their right minds." Lawson and others thought that the "invisible powers of darkness" were at work.

In Salem, Samuel Parris was one of the main supporters of the trials. He took down the statements of accused witches and tried to convince them to confess to their crimes. In September 1692, he gave a sermon describing the ongoing war between Satan and God. "If ever there were witches...here are multitudes in New England. It calls us all to mourn that the Devil had so many assistants from amongst us."

This portrait of Cotton Mather was made in the eighteenth century.

The Salem witch trials drew attention from across Massachusetts. Two men who closely followed the cases were Increase Mather and his son Cotton. Both were ministers from Boston interested in fighting witchcraft. In 1689, Cotton wrote that "evil spirits are all around. There is...a vast power or army of evil spirits under the government of a prince [Satan] who employs them in a continual opposition to the designs of God."

In June 1692, Cotton Mather and several other Puritan ministers issued a statement on the trials. They warned against using spectral evidence, since the devil could appear as the specter of someone who was not a witch. Yet Mather and the other ministers called for "the speedy and vigorous prosecution" of the accused. A month earlier, Mather had told a judge that a confession was the best proof of someone's being a witch and that he trusted the judges to know when a confession was believable. Other good proofs of guilt, he said, were a wound on a person's body that matched one seen on a specter and the discovery of "witch marks" on the body of the accused. These marks included moles, pimples, and warts that somehow looked unnatural.

Increase Mather attended some of the trials. He assured his son that the judges had other evidence besides the reports of specters that led to guilty verdicts. The younger Mather continued to support the trials, even as others began to question them.

In Their Own Words

In 1693, Cotton Mather published *Wonders of the Invisible World.*
In this book, he described and defended the Salem witch trials. Here is
a selection from that book.

*By these confessions it is agreed that the devil has made a dreadful knot
of witches in the country, and by the help of witches has dreadfully
increased that knot; that these witches have driven...their confederate
spirits to do all sorts of mischief to the neighbors.... At...witch meetings
the wretches have proceeded so far as to...consult the methods of
rooting out the Christian religion from this country, and setting up
instead...a more gross diabolism than ever the world saw before.*

Opponents of the Witch Trials

From the start, some residents of Salem questioned whether
their accused neighbors were really witches. They also thought
that the girls making the charges were lying. However, as the
trials went on, most people were afraid to oppose them since they
might be the next to be labeled as witches.

By September 1692, some people were finally speaking
out, especially against the use of spectral evidence. The Salem
judges had ignored the advice of the Mathers not to trust this
kind of evidence.

One of the strongest attacks on the trials came from Thomas
Brattle, a merchant and scientist from Boston. He wrote a long,
public letter condemning the trials. Brattle criticized some of the
kinds of evidence accepted, such as reports of specters and the so-
called "touch test." This test required the witch's victim to touch
the accused witch. Supposedly, if the accused was actually a witch,
the evil power in the victim would flow back into the accused
witch and end the victim's torment. Brattle thought the test was

unscientific and should not be allowed in court. His letter probably influenced Governor Phips's opposition to the trials.

Another strong opponent of the trials—and the Mathers—
was Robert Calef. In 1697, he wrote a detailed account of the
witch trials, hoping to prevent any future ones. Because Calef
harshly criticized the Mathers, no Boston publisher would print
the book. Calef finally published the book in London in 1700. In
it, he denounced the girls who made the first accusations as "vile
varlets" who stirred up "a blind and most bloody rage, not against
enemies...but...against as virtuous and religious as any." Calef was
one of the few people who suggested that the witch trials were
based on lies and fear, not the actions of the devil.

As time went on, Massachusetts residents began to realize
that the people executed in Salem had not been witches. In 1697,
the colony's lawmaking body, the General Court, declared a day
of atonement. Years later, the colony voted to give money to
some of the people who had been falsely accused and to the families of those who had been executed.

In Their Own Words

Here is part of Thomas Brattle's letter attacking the Salem witch trials.

*I cannot but condemn this method of the justices, of making this
touch of the hand a rule to discover witchcraft; because I am fully
persuaded that it is sorcery, and a superstitious method, and that
which we have no rule for, either from reason or religion.*

*...There are now about fifty [confessed witches] in prison...
and I cannot but tell you that my faith is strong concerning them,
that they are deluded, imposed upon, and under the influence of
some evil spirit, and therefore, unfit to [give] evidences, either
against themselves or anyone else.*

CHAPTER FIVE

The Zenger Trial

WHAT
Printer John Peter Zenger goes to trial for libel.

ISSUE
Freedom of the press

WHERE
New York City

WHEN
1735

*E*nglish law in colonial America was more limiting than the legal protection of free speech later spelled out in the U.S. Constitution. Under English rule, Americans could not openly criticize government officials and their actions if those comments might lead to social unrest. People could also be punished if their words were thought to hurt the government's reputation or weaken public support for it. Speaking or writing such words was known as seditious libel. People charged with this crime faced jail.

By the 1720s, the large colonial cities had newspapers, and they usually supported the government. In Boston, Massachusetts, and New York City, printers relied on government contracts for most of their income. They could not afford to criticize public officials if they wanted to keep their contracts. Some printers, however, were willing to publish articles written by government critics—despite the law against seditious libel. The printers either agreed with the critics or did not have government contracts and needed the work.

New York Politics

The roots of the Zenger trial started with political struggles in New York. In 1731, William Cosby took over as governor of the colony. Cosby sparked a political battle when he sued Rip Van Dam, who had briefly filled in as governor before Cosby took over. By tradition, Van Dam was supposed to share part of his salary with Cosby, but he refused.

Van Dam, who was Dutch, had the support of many wealthy Dutch residents of the colony, as well as others who felt that Cosby was threatening their economic interests. On the other side, Cosby's backers included Stephen Delancey. He and other successful merchants had done well under the last English governor, and they wanted a good relationship with Cosby, as well.

In 1733, Cosby brought his case against Van Dam to New York's Supreme Court. Most cases in the court were heard with a jury and followed English common law. This law had developed over hundreds of years through decisions made by judges in trials with juries. Cosby, however, was seen by a special form of the Supreme Court that did not use a jury. Only the court's three judges would decide the case. The chief justice was Lewis Morris. He said that the case should be heard by a jury, but the other two justices—including James Delancey, son of Stephen Delancey—disagreed.

John Peter Zenger entered the conflict when he printed Morris's statement against the Supreme Court's decision. Upset that Morris had gone public with his legal attack, Cosby removed Morris from the court. The governor then made James Delancey the new chief justice. Morris and the Delanceys had competed for power in New York politics for years. The conflict with Cosby fueled Morris's desire to take on both the governor and the Delanceys.

Two Newspapers, One Arrest

At the time, New York had just one newspaper, the *New York Gazette*. Its publisher, William Bradford, supported Cosby and would not print any attacks on him or his policies. Morris and his supporters decided to fund their own newspaper. They paid Zenger to print the *New York Weekly Journal*. Most of the paper was written by James Alexander, a lawyer who had worked for Rip Van Dam. The paper's sole focus was to criticize Cosby and praise a new political party that formed around Morris.

> *Fast Fact*
>
> Morris and his political supporters were known as the Popular Party, while Cosby and his supporters were called the Court Party.

> *Fast Fact*
>
> Common-law courts rely on precedents, or decisions made by earlier courts in similar cases, to decide their verdicts. This feature of common-law justice is still used today by all U.S. courts.

The first issue of the *Weekly Journal* appeared in November 1733. One article described Morris's victory in a local election. The reporter also pointed out that Cosby had illegally tried to prevent some people from voting.

Over the next year, the *Weekly Journal* printed attacks on Cosby and his friends. In October 1734, the governor ordered that four issues of the paper be burned because they contained many articles critical of the government. A month later, Zenger was arrested for seditious libel. His wife and servants, however, continued to print his paper.

Burning copies of the New York Weekly Journal, *was both practical and symbolic: it got rid of the offending newspapers, and it sent the message that public criticism of the government would not be tolerated.*

The Trial

Zenger sat in jail for eight months waiting for his trial. Cosby picked Chief Justice Delancey and another Court Party judge to hear the case. Delancey took control of the jury selection process, and the twelve jurors were about evenly split between Court and Popular Party members.

Zenger's lawyer was Andrew Hamilton. Hamilton was considered one of the best lawyers in colonial America. He told the jury that Zenger had published the papers said to contain seditious libel. This admission surprised everyone in the court. Under English law, the jury was supposed to decide if Zenger was indeed the printer. If he was, the jury had to find him guilty. The government lawyer, Richard Bradley, then stated what he thought was obvious: "As Mr. Hamilton has confessed the printing and publishing of these libels, I think the jury must find for the king." Chief Justice Delancey agreed.

Hamilton rejected the government's response. He convinced the jury to go against common law and find Zenger not guilty. Zenger was released the next day.

The Government's Case

In court, Hamilton tried to suggest that true statements could not be libelous; Bradley argued that English law said just the opposite: "[Indeed,] the law says their being true is an aggravation of the crime."

In his argument, Bradley said that English citizens relied on the government to protect them and their property. Public attacks on government officials could hurt their ability to carry out their jobs if the words made the public hate or distrust them. Zenger, Bradley said, had printed articles that claimed Cosby was denying New Yorkers their legal rights. That claim, whether true or false, was "stirring up...discontent among the people" and so was seditious libel. Bradley also cited the Bible to defend his position. He quoted a passage that said, "Thou shalt not speak evil of the ruler of thy people."

Chief Justice Delancey supported Bradley's interpretation of the law. He cited cases that said truth was not a defense against libel. He also instructed the jury that its only job was to decide if

Zenger had published the articles. Delancey would decide if the articles contained seditious libel.

In Their Own Words

Here is part of Richard Bradley's statements during the Zenger trial.

The case before the court is whether Mr. Zenger is guilty of libeling His Excellency the Governor of New York, and indeed the whole administration of the government. Mr. Hamilton has confessed the printing and publishing, and I think nothing is plainer than that the words...are "scandalous, and tend to sedition."... If such papers are not libels, I think it may be said there can be no such thing as libel.

Hamilton's Defense

Hamilton first focused his argument on whether Zenger had published the truth. If he had, then he did not commit seditious libel. Hamilton pointed out other English cases that seemed to say that truth could be a defense against the charge of libel. He also examined the government's own charges against Zenger. The printer was accused of publishing "a certain false, malicious, seditious, and scandalous libel." Hamilton said that "this word 'false' must have some meaning, or else how came it there?" Hamilton said that Zenger could not be guilty of libel if what he printed was true. He insisted that Bradley had to prove the words were false to show that Zenger had committed libel.

Hamilton also claimed that even if English common law might find Zenger guilty, the law was not the same in America. Over time, the colonies had changed the interpretations of some laws. In this case, libel against the governor of a colony was not the same as libeling the king.

As the trial went on, Hamilton could see that he was not winning his argument. He then used a tactic that lawyers call jury nullification. He wanted the jury to ignore the precedents and legal principles that Bradley and Delancey mentioned. Instead, Hamilton hoped that the jurors would see another principle at work in the case that would lead them to find Zenger not guilty. That principle was the right to speak and write freely about government actions. Hamilton argued that Cosby's actions had hurt the citizens of New York, and Zenger was right to complain about them.

Brilliantly defended by Andrew Hamilton, publisher John Peter Zenger was found not guilty of seditious libel. The 1734 trial marked the beginning of popular support for one of the most cherished and fundamental freedoms of citizens in what would become the United States of America: freedom of speech.

In Their Own Words

Here is part of Andrew Hamilton's speech to the jury.

It is not the cause of one poor printer, nor of New York alone, which you are now trying. No! It may in its consequence affect every free man that lives under a British government on the main of America. It is the best cause. It is the cause of liberty.... Nature and the laws of our country have given us a right to liberty of both exposing and opposing arbitrary power... by speaking and writing the truth.

After the Trial

Despite the jury's ruling in favor of Zenger, American judges and lawyers still considered seditious libel a crime, even if the statements were true. Yet some officials were less likely to arrest printers for the crime. They saw that public opinion was swinging toward greater freedom of the press. The officials did not want to risk other lawyers using jury nullification to win freedom for their clients.

News of Zenger's trial and Hamilton's defense spread throughout the colonies. The result showed that a paper—and the people—could question a royal governor's actions. Newspapers became bolder in their opinions. By the time of the American Revolution (1775–1783), many Americans realized how important the Zenger trial had been for promoting free speech in the colonies. Gouverneur Morris, grandson of Lewis Morris and a supporter of the Revolution, said that "the trial of Zenger in 1735 was the morning star of liberty which subsequently revolutionized America."

CHAPTER SIX

The Great Awakening

WHAT

American colonists pursue a renewed interest in religion.

ISSUE

*Control of religious institutions and the role of
common people in society*

WHERE

Across the colonies

WHEN

Late 1730s–1760s

*I*n colonial America, Protestantism was the dominant religious faith, and religion played a large role in daily life. Churches educated children, helped the poor, and led action on political issues. In some colonies, one type of Protestant faith was established over others—it was considered the official religion, and everyone, including nonbelievers, paid taxes to support it. Political leaders had to belong to the established church; so did anyone else who wanted to be a respected member of the community.

In the 1720s, Congregationalism was the established church in most of New England. This faith was based on the ideas of the Puritans and Pilgrims who had come to the region in the early seventeenth century. Rhode Island was a noticeable exception. Its founder, Roger Williams, had been kicked out of Massachusetts because he did not accept all Puritan teachings. His colony welcomed believers of any faith.

In most of the South, Anglicanism was the established religion, or at least the most widely practiced faith. Maryland was founded by Roman Catholics, but by the early 1700s, the Anglicans had established their religion there. Anglicans belonged to the Church of England, that country's national church. The middle colonies of New York, New Jersey, Delaware, and Pennsylvania did not have an established church, though many Quakers settled in Pennsylvania. Like Rhode Island, Pennsylvania was one of the rare colonies that eagerly accepted members of any church. Many Presbyterians also lived in the middle colonies. Their religion was similar to Congregationalism in many ways. New York and New Jersey also had members of the Dutch Reformed Church, a Protestant faith practiced by the region's original Dutch settlers.

> *Fast Fact*
>
> Few Jewish settlers lived in colonial America. By 1780, Jews had just five synagogues where they could worship. Most Jews lived in large cities, such as New York and Charleston, or in colonies that tolerated many religions, such as Rhode Island and Pennsylvania.

The First Signs
of an Awakening

The dominant Protestant faiths, whether established or not, were tied to the social and political leaders of a particular region. In some ways, the churches were conservative—they supported traditional religious beliefs and actions as they had developed in the colonies. They also supported the power of the political leaders who belonged to their churches.

For the most part, the ministers of the major Protestant churches were well educated. In their sermons, they used reason to explain why believers should accept the teachings of the Bible and live as good Christians. At this time in America, as in Europe, scientific thinking influenced many people. Scientists such as Isaac Newton were explaining how the universe worked using scientific laws, not the actions of God. Many Protestant ministers shared this increasing interest in using science to understand the natural world—and people's relation with God. As one Congregationalist minister said, "There is nothing in Christianity that is contrary to reason."

At the same time, some American ministers were taking an interest in pietism. In this form of religious experience, an individual's personal relation with God was more important than strict church rules. Pietists believed that Christians were directly touched by God in a spiritual way, converting them into true members of a church. The most important mission for a pietist minister was "saving souls": converting people into Christians so they could go to Heaven. Most ministers influenced by pietism appealed to people's emotions rather than their reason. The ministers said that society had turned away from God's teachings and that the devil was taking control of people's souls. By repenting, or asking forgiveness for their bad behavior, sinners could be saved.

Famous Figures

JONATHAN EDWARDS
(1703–1758)

Jonathan Edwards is considered one of the greatest religious thinkers in American history. He was the grandson of Solomon Stoddard, a Congregationalist minister who served in Northampton, Massachusetts for almost sixty years. Edwards studied at Yale and worked at several other churches before taking over for his grandfather in 1729. In one of his most famous sermons, "Sinners in the Hand of an Angry God," Edwards stressed the idea that humans are basically sinful and that God judges their actions before deciding who will go to Heaven. Edwards also said that God loved people and gave them a way to save themselves—by following the Bible. Edwards played a large role in spreading the Great Awakening across New England.

Around 1720, the Dutch Reformed minister Jacob Frelinghuysen began preaching pietist ideas in New Jersey. Even more influential was a Scottish Presbyterian minister, William Tennant. In 1727, he opened a small college for teaching ministers his pietist approach to his faith. His son Gilbert also played a role in shaping a new approach to Christianity in America.

In Northampton, Massachusetts, a young Congregationalist minister named Jonathan Edwards preached similar ideas. During the early 1730s, Edwards heard about Gilbert Tennant and his religious revivals in New Jersey. His pietist sermons were leading people to convert and create a more personal relationship with God. Holding his own pietist revivals, Edwards matched Tennant's success, and revivals soon spread along the lower Connecticut River valley in New England. Together, the revivals were called "the Great Awakening." In 1737, Edwards explained the results of awakenings: "They have brought [people] immediately to quit their sinful practices.... When once the Spirit of God began to be so wonderfully poured out in a general way through the town, people had soon done with their old quarrels...the tavern was soon left empty...and every day seemed in many respects like a Sabbath day."

Whitefield Fuels the Faithful

In England, a minister named George Whitefield read Edwards's writings on the revivals in New England and New Jersey. Whitefield was conducting his own revivals, and news of them had reached the colonies. In 1739, Whitefield came to America to preach, marking what most historians consider the true start of the Great Awakening.

> *Fast Fact*
>
> The first colleges founded by American colonists were associated with different Protestant religions. Two of the first three, Harvard in Massachusetts (1636) and Yale in Connecticut (1701), were Congregationalist schools. William and Mary in Virginia (1693) was Anglican. The College of New Jersey, now Princeton University, was founded in 1746 by Presbyterians. The College of Rhode Island, today known as Brown University, was started by Baptists in 1764.

Starting in Georgia, Whitefield traveled across the colonies for almost two years. He had his greatest impact in New England, reaching out mostly to Congregationalists, Presbyterians, and members of the Dutch Reformed Church. His appearances were heavily advertised, and his final sermon in Boston, Massachusetts, drew 20,000 people. Whitefield was more like a performer than a minister, using a loud, deep voice to hold his listeners' attention.

Whitefield was an itinerant, meaning he moved from town to town to preach. His revivals led many Americans to convert or renew their commitment to God. His work also led to more itinerants traveling across the colonies, trying to copy his success.

The traveling preachers added several new elements to American religion. For the first time, members of different Protestant faiths came together to hear sermons. The itinerants' messages tended to ignore the differences between the faiths and stress a common theme: saving one's soul through God. The preachers of the Great Awakening also welcomed African Americans, Native Americans, and poor whites—people not accepted in some established churches.

In the South, the revivalist movement did not pick up until several years after Whitefield's American tour. Many itinerants were Baptists, who believed that people should be baptized only after they had converted, not when they were infants. Some Baptist preachers converted during the early years of the Great Awakening and then

This portrait of itinerant preacher George Whitefield dates from about 1755.

traveled through frontier areas of Virginia and the Carolinas spreading the word of God. The main thrust of the Great Awakening lasted through the 1760s in the region. In the Northeast, however, the original strength of the movement had weakened a bit by that time.

Divisions in the Ministry

Many ministers welcomed Whitefield and his efforts to strengthen Christian faith. As the Great Awakening spread, however, some ministers began to turn away from the itinerants who came after him. Within the major churches, two groups emerged: people who supported the revivals and people who opposed them. The supporters were often called "New Lights," and their opponents were known as "Old Lights."

Not all the New Lights, however, shared the same ideas. They often split into two loose groups, known today as moderates and radicals. The moderate ministers included Jonathan Edwards and the Tennants. Although the moderates supported the value of the revival, they did not always welcome itinerants. The moderates saw a need for keeping the old church structure. Radicals, however, believed that individuals could make religious decisions on their own, without being part of a formal church. One radical said, "The common people claim as good [a] right to judge and act for themselves in matters of religion as...the learned clergy."

The radical New Light ministers were the ones who sought to convert nonwhites and the poor. Some also believed that women should be active in the revivals, and a few women actually preached—something neither moderates nor Old Lights accepted.

Fast Fact

Many ministers accepted slaves and free blacks at revivals, but they did not try to end slavery or racial inequality. During the mid-eighteenth century, the Quakers were the only religious group to oppose slavery.

The New Lights Attack the Old

To some New Lights, Old Light ministers were not converted and could not truly help others find faith in God. Some radical New Lights believed that members should leave a church if their ministers did not convert. New Light ministers often attacked the Old Lights for relying on reason and their intellect and ignoring emotions. New Lights believed that God, through the Holy Spirit, stirred converts to shout, sing, and move about. Old Lights thought that sermons should stir deep thoughts, not such physical outbursts.

One of the most radical New Lights was James Davenport. He preached that people should not attend religious services given by unconverted ministers. Davenport also protested against laws that tried to restrict itinerants. During one famous sermon, he had his followers burn items that were considered unholy. Included in the flames were articles written by Old Light ministers who opposed Davenport.

In some communities, New Lights formed their own churches, taking converted members from the established churches. These "Separates" sometimes refused to pay taxes to support the established churches. One Separate minister wrote that old churches put too much stress on a person's good behavior, rather than on the need for converting. The old churches also let nonbelievers worship with true believers. These nonbelievers, he wrote, "are awful mockers at the spirit of God, and the saints that are under the influence of that same spirit." Separating from those people was the only way to create a real church devoted to God. Some Separates also complained because their regular ministers would not let itinerants speak in their church.

In Their Own Words

In 1740, Gilbert Tennant gave a sermon attacking unconverted ministers. Here is some of what he said.

They have not the courage, or honesty, to thrust the nail of terror into sleeping souls; nay, sometimes they strive with all their might to fasten terror into the hearts of the righteous, and so to make those sad whom GOD would not have made sad!… 'Isn't an unconverted minister like a man who would learn others to swim before he has learned it himself, and so is drowned in the act and dies like a fool?'

The Old Lights' Concerns

To some Old Light ministers, the Great Awakening was a threat to their leadership. The revivalists said that individuals had the power to find God and lead a moral life on their own. The New Lights often took away the established churches' members, and people who did stay in those churches questioned the ministers who did not embrace the revivalist ways.

One of the leading critics of the New Lights was Charles Chauncy, a Congregationalist minister from Boston. Chauncy thought that the revivalists preached superstition, not Christianity, and stirred wild emotions in their followers. Converted ministers often did not have any formal education, and Old Lights questioned their ability to understand the Bible or religious thought. Chauncy also believed that once an itinerant minister left a town, most of the "converts" went back to their sinful ways.

Some opponents of the Great Awakening feared that attacks on religious tradition and order would spill

Fast Fact

In New England, many Separates eventually joined the Baptist Church. The Baptists had first formed in England in the early seventeenth century. For decades, they could not freely practice their faith in colonial America. The Great Awakening increased the number of Baptist churches in America.

over into politics and other parts of society. These critics did not want radical ideas to spread into those areas of life.

To some Old Lights, the revivals themselves were radical. The events brought together young men and women and encouraged them to share their emotions with each other. Traditional ministers looked down on this mixing of the sexes in public. At the revivals, newly converted believers sometimes confessed their sins. Old Lights did not approve of hearing the details of these acts.

Over time, relations between moderate New Lights and Old Lights began to improve. The Old Lights could not stop the growth of new churches and the training of ministers who stressed conversions. The two groups realized that they had enough in common to work together—and try to limit the influence of the radical New Lights. Old Light ministers also began to give church members more power in running their congregations. The Great Awakening also made pietism a permanent part of religious life in America.

In Their Own Words

Here is part of a letter, written in 1742, in which Charles Chauncy criticized revivalism.

The goodness that has been so much talked of…is nothing more, in general, than a commotion in the passions…. 'Tis not evident to me that persons, generally, have a better understanding of religion, a better government of their passions, a more Christian love to their neighbor, or that they are more decent and regular in their devotions toward God…. They too much neglect their reason and judgment.

CHAPTER SEVEN

The Stamp Act Crisis

WHAT

A British attempt to tax all public papers and documents
stirs colonial anger.

ISSUE

Taxation without representation in the government

WHERE

Across the thirteen American colonies

WHEN

1765–1766

*A*fter its victory in the French and Indian War (1754–1763), Great Britain faced an economic crisis. The country was deeply in debt, and it would need even more money to station troops in its expanded North American empire.

Parliament is the British lawmaking body, and the most important position in Parliament is prime minister. In 1763, George Grenville held that job, and he was determined to make the American colonies pay their fair share of their military defense. Even before Grenville came to power, Parliament had taken several steps to strengthen its control over the colonies. The British particularly wanted to enforce the collection of duties, taxes paid on goods brought into the colonies from overseas. For decades, the Americans had smuggled in many items to avoid paying the duties.

King George III and Grenville began crafting new policies designed to limit the actions of the colonists. The Proclamation of 1763 said that the Americans could not settle in lands west of the Allegheny Mountains, which stretch from present-day Pennsylvania to West Virginia. Some Americans had already moved there, and more planned to buy land in the region for future sale. Investors and settlers resented this British attempt to limit their movements.

The next year, Grenville passed a new law that tackled the smuggling of a key product: molasses. The colonies bought molasses from the sugar-producing islands of the West Indies and then turned it into rum. To avoid a duty on molasses, shippers had been smuggling it for decades, and the British had not actively tried to stop them. Under the new Revenue Act (also called the Sugar Act), Grenville reduced the duty on molasses from six pence to three pence per gallon. He hoped that Americans would be more willing to pay the lower duty. At the same time, the British increased their efforts to catch smugglers and actually collect the money.

Americans in several colonies disliked this new effort to collect the duty, and they protested against the Sugar Act. In Newport, Rhode Island, town residents fired a cannon at a ship sent to collect duties. Massachusetts leaders claimed that the colonies would have "no liberty, no happiness, no security," if the British taxed them in this way. Grenville, ignoring the protests, prepared an even more sweeping tax plan for the colonies.

Famous Figures

GEORGE GRENVILLE
(1712–1770)

Trained as a lawyer, George Grenville came from a well-known English family. He entered Parliament in 1741 and became prime minister to King George III in 1763. Grenville had almost no interest in the American colonies before taking over as prime minister, and in that position, he largely ignored the colonists' concerns about their legal rights. Grenville stepped down as prime minister in 1765, but he continued to defend his forceful policies against the colonies.

The Stamp Act

In Great Britain, citizens paid a tax on almost every public document. To show that the tax had been paid, a stamp was affixed to the document. Even as Grenville was putting the Sugar Act in place, he was making plans to bring the stamp tax to the colonies.

The Stamp Act of 1765 required the colonists to pay a tax on legal papers, newspapers, contracts, and even playing cards. The tax was so broad that almost all classes of society were affected, from the wealthy to poor workers. The new tax was especially hard on the colonists because it had to be paid in silver, and silver coins were difficult to acquire in the colonies. Anyone arrested for not paying the tax went to trial in a special court, which did not use a jury.

Through the spring and summer of 1765, the British government selected commissioners to collect the stamp tax in each colony. The colonists protested against the tax—sometimes violently. In Boston, Massachusetts, on August 14, protesters tied an effigy, or dummy, to a tree. The effigy represented Andrew Oliver, the new tax commissioner for the colony. When a sheriff tried to cut down "Oliver," thousands of protesters threatened him. By the end of the day, the protesters had cut down the effigy, cut off its head, and burned it. They then marched through Boston and destroyed a new shop that Oliver had just built. Next, the mob headed for Oliver's house, intending to beat him up—or perhaps kill him. The tax commissioner was not there, so the protesters wrecked the house. The following day, Oliver quit his job as tax commissioner.

This engraving depicts a riot against the stamp tax. The banner carried by the protesters refers to the Stamp Act as "The Folly of England and the Ruin of America."

Violence erupted again in Boston a few weeks later. This time, the protesters stormed the house of Lieutenant Governor Thomas Hutchinson. As one eyewitness described the scene, the crowd "destroyed windows, doors, furniture...and paintings, and stole...cash as well as clothing and silverware."

The protests also spread to other colonies. The protesters called themselves "the Sons of Liberty." The name came from a speech given in Parliament by one of the few lawmakers who strongly supported the colonists. With the Sons ready to use violence, tax commissioners feared for their lives. By November, none of the colonies had a commissioner willing to try to collect the stamp tax.

Political and business interests in the colonies also took action against the tax. In October, nine colonies sent representatives to a meeting in New York called the Stamp Act Congress. The members of the congress insisted that they were loyal to King George III but that the colonies could not be taxed without representation. After the congress, merchants agreed not to buy goods from Great Britain. The Americans hoped to hurt the British economy and convince Parliament to remove the tax.

> *Fast Fact*
>
> During the late 1760s in several American cities, groups of women formed the Daughters of Liberty. The Daughters met to spin yarn and weave cloth so that Americans would not have to buy clothes from Great Britain.

Ending the Stamp Tax

In England, some merchants also complained about the new tax on the Americans. Due to the American refusal to import goods from Great Britain, merchants were losing money. By the beginning of 1766, Charles Watson-Wentworth, also called Lord Rockingham, had become prime minister. Rockingham was eager to repeal the Stamp Act. Some members of Parliament, however, still favored the tax.

As Parliament debated repealing the tax, it heard from many people who knew about the situation in America. One of the most prominent was Benjamin Franklin. Franklin served as an agent for several American colonies, representing their interests in London, the capital of England. Franklin explained that the colonists already paid a number of taxes. He also noted that, before 1763, Americans "had not only a respect, but an affection for, Great Britain, for its laws, its customs and manners." The laws passed since then, he said, had "greatly lessened" American respect for Parliament.

Famous Figures

BENJAMIN FRANKLIN
(1706–1790)

Benjamin Franklin was already a well-known writer and scientist when he took the job as colonial agent for Pennsylvania. Born in Boston, Franklin moved to Philadelphia, Pennsylvania, as a young man and became one of the city's most respected residents. He helped found the city's first fire department and its first library. As a publisher, he was famous for *Poor Richard's Almanac*, a listing of weather information and wise sayings.

Before the Stamp Act crisis, Franklin was a dedicated British citizen. By the time the tax was repealed, he was certain that the colonies would one day have to demand their independence. In 1776, Franklin served on the committee that wrote the Declaration of Independence. For most of the American Revolution (1775–1783), he was America's leading diplomat in France. Franklin played a key role in winning French support for the Revolution. Franklin served his country again in 1787 when he helped to create the U.S. Constitution.

American Arguments against the Stamp Act

Almost as soon as they learned about the Stamp Act, some Americans began to protest. One of the first was Virginia lawmaker Patrick Henry. He said that Parliament did not have a right to collect this tax. Henry and others claimed that since the colonies had no representatives in Parliament, they could not be taxed. No one in that lawmaking body represented their interests. This idea quickly spread throughout the colonies, and some Americans cried, "Taxation without representation is tyranny."

By this time, many colonists were making a distinction between what were called external and internal taxes. Americans agreed that Parliament could pass external taxes, such as duties. Trade was an external affair—something outside the colonies—and Parliament was responsible for controlling external activities for all of Great Britain. The stamp tax, however, affected internal events, or activities within the colonies. An internal tax, they argued, was illegal if the colonies did not have representatives in Parliament who could help shape the tax or fight against it.

The feelings against the Stamp Act were not all based on deep political beliefs. Some Americans simply did not want to pay any taxes to Parliament. Additionally, some of the protesters welcomed an excuse to riot or steal from people who worked for the British government. In Boston, many of the protesters were sailors and young men without jobs. They belonged to gangs that controlled the city's waterfront. Several leaders in Boston recruited the gangs to attack colonial officials in the city. Patriots such as John Adams criticized this kind of mob violence, even as they attacked the Stamp Act. (Patriots were colonists who opposed British efforts to limit American freedom.)

In Their Own Words

In October 1765, the Stamp Act Congress issued a declaration of colonial rights and complaints against Parliament. Here is part of that declaration.

[It] is inseparably essential to the freedom of a people, and the undoubted rights of Englishmen, that no taxes should be imposed on them, but with their own consent, or by their representatives.... The people of these colonies are not...represented in the [Parliament] of Great Britain.... The only representatives of the people of these colonies are persons chosen therein, by themselves; and...no taxes ever have been, or can be, constitutionally imposed on them, but by their respective legislatures.

The British Arguments for the Tax

Many members of the British Parliament rejected the arguments against taxation without representation. They claimed that the colonists had "virtual" representation. Parliament, as a whole, represented the interests of all British citizens. The Americans did not vote for a representative, but most residents of England, Scotland, and Ireland could not vote either. All were "virtually" represented by the lawmakers chosen by the small number of people who could vote. Most Americans could not accept this argument. As James Otis wrote, the same logic might lead the British to say "that [Parliament] in fact represent[s] all the people of the globe."

George Grenville, still a member of Parliament, led a group that opposed repealing the Stamp Act. He accepted the notion of virtual representation, and he insisted that Parliament had a right to collect internal taxes in America. The former prime minister even suggested sending the military to America to end the protests and force the colonists to pay the tax.

Some British did not directly address the issue of taxation without representation. Instead, they focused on how much Great Britain had done for the colonies. In London, a newspaper writer using the name William Pym offered these views against the Americans: "They know very well that a great part of our national debt was contracted in establishing them on a firm foundation, and protecting them from...enemies.—Can then anything be so unreasonable as a refusal of their assistance to wipe out a little of [the debt]?"

This cartoon from a colonial newspaper depicts the repeal of the one-year-old Stamp Act as the funeral of a child (the fourth man in the procession carries a small casket).

The End of the Crisis

In March 1766, Parliament repealed the Stamp Act, but it also passed the Declaratory Act. In this new law, Parliament said it had the "full power and authority to make laws...to bind the colonies and people of America." Franklin thought that the Declaratory Act was just for "appearances." He wrote to Pennsylvania leaders, "I think we may rest secure...that no future Ministry will ever attempt to tax us again." Franklin, however, was wrong. Parliament had backed down on the Stamp Act, but it still insisted that it had absolute control over the colonies. Parliament claimed the right to collect future taxes without giving the Americans representation.

In America, many colonists celebrated the repeal of the Stamp Act. Their happiness, however, did not mean that they accepted Parliament's right to pass future taxes. Over the next few years, the British continued to find ways to raise money in the colonies. The Americans continued to speak against taxation without representation. The Stamp Act marked a turning point in the relations between the colonies and Great Britain. Parliament was determined not to seem weak, while the Americans believed they had to speak out more loudly against threats to their rights.

In Their Own Words

One supporter of virtual representation was Soame Jenyns, a member of Parliament. Here is part of what he wrote during the Stamp Act crisis.

[Many] more of our richest and most flourishing trading towns send no members to Parliament, consequently they cannot consent by their representatives because they choose none to represent them. Yet are they not Englishmen? Or are they not taxed?...Why does not this imaginary representation extend to America as well as over the whole island of Great Britain?... Are [Americans] not Englishmen? Or are they only Englishmen when they solicit protection, but not Englishmen when taxes are required to enable this country to protect them?

CHAPTER EIGHT

The Coming of the American Revolution

WHAT

American and British troops fight the first battles
of the American Revolution.

ISSUE

The need for armed conflict against Great Britain

WHERE

In the Massachusetts towns of Lexington and Concord

WHEN

1775

*I*n the fall of 1774, tensions were high in and around Boston, Massachusetts. Throughout the region, Patriots practiced their military skills and acquired weapons, preparing for a future battle with British troops stationed in the area. (Patriots were colonists who opposed British efforts to limit American freedom.) Both sides sensed that violence could break out at any time.

Since 1765, Boston had been the center of Patriot protests against British taxes and laws that seemed to weaken American freedoms. King George III was determined to show the Americans that they could not defy his authority. In 1768, he sent the first British troops into Boston. In 1770, their presence sparked the Boston Massacre, in which the troops fired on a crowd of Americans threatening a British guard, leading to the deaths of five of the Americans. Afterward, the British moved their military forces to an island in Boston Harbor. Following the Boston Tea Party of 1773, King George sent more troops to Boston. Parliament, the British lawmaking body, also passed new laws that gave the British government more control over Massachusetts. The British called these laws the Coercive Acts, but the Americans referred to them as the Intolerable Acts.

The British commander in Boston—and the new governor of Massachusetts—was General Thomas Gage, a veteran of the French and Indian War (1754–1763) who had also served as the commander in chief of all British forces in North America. Under Gage, the British troops controlled Boston, shutting down the harbor and trying to enforce the Intolerable Acts. Many residents left the city rather than face the strict military rule. Residents who stayed behind were forced to house and feed the troops.

Strong reaction to the British moves in Boston spread across the colonies. Residents in Kingston, New Hampshire, sent a letter offering their support, noting that "we look on the cause in which you are engaged as a common cause" and calling the British soldiers "unjust invaders." Kingston, like many other towns, also sent food to ease shortages in Boston. Among the items sent were sheep, wheat, corn, and bread.

The colonial response also included political and economic action. In September 1774, representatives from every colony but Georgia met in Philadelphia, Pennsylvania, for the First Continental Congress. Georgia decided not to send any representatives because of their loyalty to the king. During the next several weeks, they debated what to do. In the end, the congress approved a statement that called for the protection of such rights as "life, liberty, and property" and for the colonies alone to have power over their own taxation. The congress also called for cutting off all trade with Great Britain.

THE BOSTON TEA PARTY

In 1773, Great Britain removed all the taxes it had placed on colonial goods—except for one on tea. To protest the tea tax, Patriots in Boston dressed as Native Americans and raided three British ships docked in the harbor. The raiders threw more than 300 chests of tea into the water. This "Boston Tea Party" put the colonies and Great Britain farther along the path to war.

Preparing for War

Even before he learned about the American demands, King George was ready for war. "The New England governments are in a state of rebellion," he wrote his prime minister, Lord North, in November 1774. "Blows (warfare) must decide whether they are to be subject to this country or independent."

In Massachusetts, Gage knew about the military training going on in and around Boston. Some local militias were meeting several times a week, and a number of towns, such as Concord, northwest of Boston, had formed special units called Minutemen. As the name suggests, these soldiers were supposed to be ready to fight with just one minute's notice.

By December, Gage was calling for more troops. He had only 3,000 soldiers in Boston. He needed, he wrote to London, "a sufficient force to command the country by marching into it." Earlier, he had said that if Parliament thought 10,000 troops would be enough, it should send twice as many just to be safe.

THE BIRTH OF THE MINUTEMEN

Worcester, Massachusetts, could be called the birthplace of the Revolutionary Minutemen. The term had already been in use for about twenty years, but in September 1774, the Worcester militia set up the model for these special forces that other towns followed. Usually, about one-quarter to one-third of the regular militia were recruited to serve as Minutemen. Most were young farmers or craftsmen. The Minutemen elected their officers, some of whom had fought in the French and Indian War. After the battles at Lexington and Concord, other colonies formed their own Minutemen units, though the Massachusetts Minutemen became part of George Washington's Continental Army.

On the Road to Lexington and Concord

As 1775 began, the Boston region was fairly quiet, but Parliament was once again focusing on the political troubles there. In early February, Lord North and his allies passed a resolution stating that Massachusetts was in a state of rebellion. The government made plans to send more troops to Boston—though fewer than Gage had requested. In Parliament, one British lawmaker called the Americans "raw, undisciplined, cowardly men." He and others seemed sure that Great Britain could easily defeat any Patriot army if fighting broke out.

On April 14, Gage received a letter from London. His instructions were to arrest the Patriot leaders in Massachusetts and take "decisive" action to end the rebellion. The next day, a spy reported that Patriot leaders were planning to ask the other New England colonies to form an army. Gage also knew that the Patriots had amassed a large amount of gunpowder in Concord. The general decided it was time to act. He prepared to send troops to Concord.

Gage assembled a force of about 800 men to march to Concord and seize the gunpowder there. They were also ordered to arrest two of the Patriot leaders, Samuel Adams and John Hancock. The British "Regulars," as the colonists called them, left Boston on the night of April 18.

Patriots in the city knew that the British were planning to move. One of the American leaders, Joseph Warren, sent Paul Revere and William Dawes to alert Adams and Hancock that the British might be coming for them. The two Patriots were staying in Lexington. Revere, one of the leaders of the local Sons of Liberty, later described how he evaded two British soldiers on the road and then headed for the town of Medford. There, he wrote, "I awaked the captain of the minute men; and after that, I alarmed almost every house, till I got to Lexington."

After reaching Lexington around midnight, Revere and Dawes headed for Concord. Joined by a third rider, Samuel Prescott, they were stopped by a British patrol. Prescott made a break and escaped, riding on to Concord. Revere was questioned and then let go, while Dawes returned to Boston.

As the morning went on, church bells rang out across the countryside, warning people that the British were coming. Before dawn, Minutemen and militiamen gathered at the Lexington town green, ready for battle. Leading them was Captain John Parker, a Minuteman.

*Minutemen were members of special units from various colonial militias
who were recruited to be ready to fight at a moment's notice. Although the term
"Minutemen" was widely used, it was the Massachusetts Minutemen who gained
renown in the early battles of the Revolution. Eventually they became part of
George Washington's Continental Army.*

The Americans in Lexington were badly outnumbered. When the British commander ordered the Patriots to disperse, Parker instructed his men to do so. Then, in a confusing period of shouting and activity, someone fired a gun. (Historians still cannot say for sure which side fired the shot.) The Regulars responded by shooting at the Americans, and the Minutemen returned the fire. The British commander ordered his men to stop, but as another officer later said, "The men were so wild, they could hear no orders." Finally, the British put down their guns, leaving about twenty Americans dead or wounded. Then the British marched on to Concord, as originally planned.

The residents of Concord had hidden most of the supplies that the British were coming to capture. As the troops searched the town, the local militia set up on high ground that overlooked the main road. Then the Americans marched back toward town and met a small group of British soldiers by a bridge. The British fired warning shots, but the Americans did not stop. The British aimed at the Americans, killing and wounding several of them. As in Lexington, the militia returned fire. This time they killed several British troops. After a few minutes, the British retreated from the bridge.

The Bloodiest Part of the Battle

The Americans did not follow the British troops as they moved into Concord to rejoin the rest of the British force. However, at some point the British would have to march back to Boston, and the Americans planned to be ready.

British troops in the eighteenth century were used to fighting in an orderly way. Enemy forces usually faced each other in open fields and then marched into battle. The British preferred to fight at close quarters; they were trained to use the bayonets attached to the ends of their guns. For the most part, they were not accurate shooters.

The Americans, on the other hand, tended to be much better shots. They also used different tactics than the British. Instead of fighting in the open, they preferred to shoot from behind trees, walls, rocks, or the windows of houses. As the British marched out of Concord back toward Boston, these tactics gave the Americans the advantage. A British lieutenant described the scene: "They were so concealed there was hardly any seeing them. In this way we marched 9 and 10 miles [14 and 16 kilometers], their numbers increasing from all parts, while ours was reduced by death, wounds, and fatigue."

Although American militiamen were greatly outnumbered by British regulars at Lexington and Concord, they used battle tactics unfamiliar to the formally trained British to hold their ground and severely damage the British forces. This engraving, in which American soldiers attack their surprised enemies, shows the Battle of Lexington.

As the afternoon went on, the British tired and began to run out of ammunition; their commander feared that his troops would not make it back to Boston. Only the arrival of reinforcements ended the slaughter. That evening, the Regulars finally reached Boston. The Americans had been unable to destroy the force, but they had caused heavy damage. The British casualties that day were over 250, more than twice as many as the Americans suffered.

The Call for War

The American decision to challenge the British after the Intolerable Acts had not been clear-cut. The statement issued by members of the First Continental Congress did not necessarily reflect the thinking of all Americans. In each colony, Patriots tended to control the conventions that chose the representatives. People who supported British policies were generally left out of the process.

Even the members of the congress did not always agree on what to do. Massachusetts representatives, such as cousins Samuel Adams and John Adams, believed that the colonies would have to fight the British—and should, to win their independence. Patrick Henry was another of the "radicals" who wanted an all-out war. More moderate members, such as John Jay and Joseph Galloway, were not ready to take this bold step.

Since Massachusetts was facing the threat of British troops, its representatives played an important role at the congress. Samuel Adams wanted to make sure that the congress supported Massachusetts. John Adams realized that many colonists were not prepared to challenge the British and risk a war. He believed that the radicals had to act with "great delicacy and caution" to win support and not scare off the more moderate members.

Fast Fact

British troops marched into battle with fife-and-drum bands. On the afternoon of April 19, the British played "Yankee Doodle," a song written to make fun of the American colonists. Americans wrote their own words for the tune and sang "Yankee Doodle" throughout the war.

Famous Figures

SAMUEL ADAMS
(1722–1803)

With a flair for inciting others to take action, Samuel Adams was one of the most important Patriot leaders in the years before the American Revolution (1775–1783). Adams was the cousin of John Adams, a great political thinker who became the second president of the United States.

In 1765, Samuel Adams won a seat in the Massachusetts General Court, the colony's lawmaking body. That same year, he helped form the Sons of Liberty and emerged as a vocal opponent of the Stamp Act. In the years leading up to the Revolution, he continued to denounce British policies in the colonies, though he did not play a large role in the U.S. government after 1776.

In Their Own Words

As the First Continental Congress met, Samuel Adams wrote a letter to George Washington, one of the representatives from Virginia. Adams outlined how the citizens of Massachusetts were preparing for war.

I have written to some of our friends to provide themselves without delay...with arms and ammunition, to get well instructed in the military art...and prepare a complete set of rules, that they may be ready in case they are called to defend themselves against the violent attacks of despotism.

Seeking a Peaceful Solution

During the congress, Joseph Galloway emerged as the leader of the moderates. He knew that Samuel Adams was his primary opponent, the man who most wanted a war. Galloway believed that Adams was "by no means remarkable for brilliant abilities," but was skilled in "popular intrigue and the management of a faction." Galloway also thought that Adams was using events outside of Philadelphia to influence the debate. In mid-September, Paul Revere arrived from Boston. He carried the Suffolk Resolves—statements of proposed action written by political leaders in Boston and the rest of Suffolk County, Massachusetts. The resolves hinted at the need for war.

Samuel Adams and other radicals convinced the congress to accept the Suffolk Resolves. Galloway, however, had his own proposal, called the Plan of Union. Galloway said that he opposed British taxes on America and wanted to protect American freedom. However, he also believed that America needed a strong relationship with Great Britain to survive. Under his plan, the Americans would establish a "Grand Council" that included members from each colony. The council would be able to reject British laws that affected the colonies, except ones relating to foreign trade.

At first, Galloway's plan won support in the congress. One member said it was "almost perfect." The radicals, however, opposed it, because Parliament would still have the power to overturn the actions of the Grand Council. After a long debate, the members voted on whether or not to further consider the plan. Galloway and his supporters lost by one vote. Later, when Galloway was absent, Samuel Adams won a vote to get rid of all the records of the debate over the Plan of Union.

In Their Own Words

Even in Massachusetts, some citizens tried to fight the growing call for rebellion. Daniel Leonard, a lawyer, wrote a series of newspaper articles on the subject. Here are some of his views.

Our patriots have been so intent upon building up American rights that they have overlooked the rights of Great Britain and our own interest.... They have been arguing away our most essential rights.... It is our highest interest to continue a part of the British Empire, and equally our duty to remain subject to the authority of Parliament.

The Results of the Congress

The radicals won the key debates at the First Continental Congress. The other colonies were prepared to help Massachusetts and even go to war if necessary. However, the members made it clear that they would not fight for the colony if Americans fired first. After the battles at Lexington and Concord, Adams and other Sons of Liberty always stressed that the British had indeed fired the first shot, even though there is no proof for the claim. On April 19, 1775, the militia and Minutemen were clearly prepared for war. One historian even suggests that they had set a trap for the British Regulars who had marched out of Boston.

After Lexington and Concord, more Americans were ready to fight the British and defend liberty. Galloway was not one of them. He refused to attend the Second Continental Congress, which met in May 1775. He became one of the leading Loyalists. As many as one-third of all Americans were Loyalists throughout the war.

Famous Figures

JOSEPH GALLOWAY
(1731–1803)

A wealthy Philadelphia merchant, Joseph Galloway was a good friend of Benjamin Franklin. He was also one of the most important politicians in Pennsylvania at the time of the First Continental Congress. Once the American Revolution started, he became a leading Loyalist—an American opposed to independence. He moved to London, England, in 1778, and after the war, Pennsylvania leaders refused to let him return.

OPPOSING VIEWS IN GREAT BRITAIN

After Lexington and Concord, Parliament sent 5,000 fresh troops to Boston, and more soon followed. Not all British lawmakers, however, wanted war with the colonies. Earlier in 1775, William Pitt and Edmund Burke, two leading members of Parliament, called for a peaceful solution. Pitt said that the Intolerable Acts should be repealed. Burke said that Parliament had the right to tax the Americans. Asserting that right through war, however, would destroy Britain's relationship with the colonies. Burke thought that preserving this relationship should be Parliament's top concern.

CHAPTER NINE

The Declaration of Independence

WHAT
The Continental Congress declares American independence from Great Britain.

ISSUE
Whether America would benefit from independence

WHERE
Philadelphia, Pennsylvania

WHEN
1776

In May 1775, political representatives from every colony except Georgia met in Philadelphia, Pennsylvania, for the Second Continental Congress. At the First Continental Congress, held in the fall of 1774, the congress had agreed to support Massachusetts in its struggle against Great Britain. British troops controlled Boston, the capital of Massachusetts, and local government authority had been sharply limited by Parliament, the British lawmaking body. The First Continental Congress declared that the colonies wanted protection of their political rights. The members also said that if Great Britain attacked Massachusetts residents, the colonies would unite to help them fight back.

Fighting broke out in Massachusetts on April 19, 1775. British soldiers sent to capture arms and gunpowder exchanged shots with militiamen in Lexington and Concord. When the day was over, more than 250 British soldiers had been killed or wounded. Now, as the congress met for the second time, it faced important decisions. With no other political system in place, the congress had to serve as the national government for the united colonies.

After the fighting in April, militia from across New England traveled to the Boston area, eager to fight the British. In early June, Massachusetts asked the congress to take control of this army, which was soon known as the Continental Army. The congress chose George Washington to lead the army, which fought the British in Boston until March 1776. Next, the congress began working on a public statement defending the colonies' use of force.

John Dickinson of Pennsylvania and Thomas Jefferson of Virginia were chosen to write this document. In the "Declaration of the Causes and Necessity of Taking Up Arms," they wrote, "Honour, justice, and humanity forbid us tamely to surrender that freedom which we have received from our gallant ancestors." Yet the two men—and most of the other representatives who had gathered in Philadelphia—did not want to end America's ties to Great Britain.

Famous Figures

JOHN DICKINSON
(1732–1808)

Born in Maryland and raised in Delaware, John Dickinson eventually settled in Philadelphia and worked as a lawyer. In 1768, he wrote *Letters from a Pennsylvania Farmer,* outlining his arguments against new taxes on the colonies. This series of letters made Dickinson a popular Patriot leader. (Patriots were colonists who opposed British efforts to limit American freedom.) In 1776, he opposed the Declaration of Independence, but he remained in the Continental Congress, representing Delaware. In 1787, he attended the Constitutional Convention and supported the new national government created there.

The King Responds

Just two days after approving Jefferson and Dickinson's document, the congress drafted a letter to King George III. Officially, the document was a petition—a call for the king to take action. The members of the Continental Congress wanted George III to use his power to end the government policies that had led to the rebellion now under way. They praised George's "wise considerations" and assured him they were "faithful Colonists" eager to stay in the British Empire.

In November, the congress learned that George III had rejected its petition. It also learned that the king had declared the colonies in an official state of rebellion. From then on, British political and military officials in America could do whatever was needed to "suppress such rebellion, and to bring the traitors to justice."

In the next few months, the British showed how determined they were to end the rebellion. More troops

Fast Fact

The petition from the congress to George III was called "the Olive Branch Petition." In ancient Greece, holding out an olive branch indicated a desire to seek peace.

Fast Fact

A few months before the British attack on Norfolk, Virginia, British ships fired on Falmouth (now Portland), Maine. The British commander warned the residents before he started firing, so no one was killed, but hundreds of buildings were destroyed.

came to America, and in January 1776, a British force destroyed Norfolk, Virginia. The next month, the congress heard about the Prohibitory Act, which Parliament had passed the previous December. The law cut off all trade with the colonies and said that Britain could seize any American ship—at sea or in port—and force its sailors to join the British navy. John Adams said that, with this law, George III and Parliament had thrown "thirteen colonies out of the royal protection" and almost forced America to declare its independence.

Declaring Independence

With Great Britain building up its military force in North America, the Continental Congress finally decided to act. In June, Richard Henry Lee of Virginia introduced a resolution that reflected the thinking of many of the representatives. "These united colonies," Lee said, "are, and of right ought to be, free and independent states." The congress, however, could not yet vote on whether to support Lee's resolution. Representatives from several colonies needed instructions from their leaders on how to vote.

As the congress waited for these instructions to come, it created a committee to write a declaration of independence. If Lee's resolution was approved, this document would explain the congress's reasons for declaring independence. The congress chose five representatives to write the declaration: John Adams, Benjamin Franklin, Thomas Jefferson, Robert Livingston, and Roger Sherman. This committee of five then picked Jefferson to write the first draft of the document.

Jefferson spent several weeks writing the declaration, crossing out words and adding new ones over and over. When he was done, he gave it to the rest of the committee to review. On June 28, Jefferson brought the declaration to the congress. The next day, the representatives learned that a huge British fleet was about to land in New York. Charleston, South Carolina, had already come under attack, and a recent American invasion of Canada had failed badly.

On July 1, the congress began debating independence, and the next day, it voted to approve Lee's resolution. Then the representatives went over Jefferson's declaration, making changes so that every colony would accept the document. For example, Jefferson had criticized George III for allowing slavery in the colonies. Southern colonies, which relied heavily on slavery for their farming, did not want slavery mentioned in the declaration. Some New Englanders also opposed bringing up slavery, since sea captains from their colonies made money on the slave trade. With the changes made, each colony voted on July 4 to accept the Declaration of Independence as it stands today. With that act, the colonies became "united states of America."

On July 8, the declaration was read in public for the first time. Adams noted that the bells in Philadelphia "rang all day and almost all night," and one resident wrote that there were "great demonstrations of joy upon the unanimity of the Declaration." Copies of the document were then sent to the other states, and each reading of the declaration led to more celebrations.

Fast Fact

In New York, George Washington's troops tore down a statue of George III after hearing the Declaration of Independence. Its metal was later melted down for bullets.

The Debate for Independence

The celebrations for independence through the summer of 1776 did not include all Americans. In each state, some people remained loyal to the British. Others wanted to continue protesting British policies but still hoped for reconciliation—solving the differences between the two sides so that America would remain part of Great Britain. The calls for independence, however, eventually proved stronger than these other points of view.

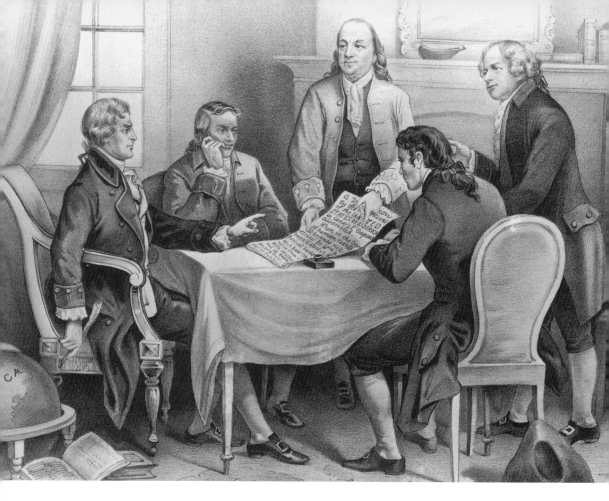

Ever since the First Continental Congress, the idea of independence had been in the air, but initially, its supporters were outnumbered by people who hoped for reconciliation. The coming of war, after April 1775, sparked more support for independence in New England. In other colonies, however—especially Pennsylvania—leaders such as Joseph Galloway were not convinced that independence would work. The colonies had different interests; how well could they work together as a nation? How would these united colonies defend themselves against the British and other European powers?

By the summer of 1775, some of the leading Patriots outside of New England were also considering independence. Acting on his own, Benjamin Franklin wrote a declaration of independence. He accused Parliament of "open robbery" of the colonies. Most of the other members of the Continental Congress did not want even to discuss the idea.

The support for independence grew as George III and Parliament took stronger military actions against the colonies. In November 1775, Thomas Jefferson wrote that he would love for America and Great Britain to remain united. "But, by the God that made me, I will cease to exist before I yield to a connection on such terms as the British Parliament propose." A few months later, General Nathanael Greene wrote from the battle-field to a member of the congress that the time for talk was over. The congress had to declare independence because "our whole property...our liberty, nay! life itself is at stake."

The debate for independence reached new heights in January 1776 when a recent English immigrant named Thomas Paine published a pamphlet called *Common Sense*. He declared that independence was the only path that America could follow to guarantee its freedom. In simple, emotional language, he argued that the nature of the British government was flawed. It rested on monarchy, the rule of kings or queens, and hereditary rule, power passed from monarchs to their children. Paine wrote that "a thirst for absolute power is the natural disease of monarchy." He also attacked hereditary rule. Like other American and British thinkers of the day, Paine believed that "all men [were] originally equal." The children of a ruler did not possess any special quality that would make them better rulers than anyone else.

Published in Philadelphia, *Common Sense* soon appeared throughout the colonies, selling tens of thousands of copies. Paine's arguments were not new. Members of the Continental Congress and newspaper publishers had written similar things about independence. However, Paine brought all those argu-ments together in one place. He also wrote specifically for the average American, not lawyers, ministers, or other educated

Fast Fact

Jefferson was chosen to write the declara-tion because of his writing skills and because he came from Virginia. The committee wanted to show that the support for independence spread beyond New England to the Southern colonies.

people. Paine's words stirred Americans who were considering independence but still had doubts. "The country was ripe for independence," one minister wrote, "and only needed somebody to tell the people so, with decision [and] boldness." George Washington wrote, "I find *Common Sense* is working a powerful change in the minds of men."

Through the spring of 1776, more Americans spoke out for independence. Some noted that the British had "lost their love of freedom." In the Continental Congress, John Adams was one of the leading supporters of independence. Cutting all ties with Britain, he believed, would lead to better government in America. It would also make it easier for the colonies to fight their war against Great Britain. He believed that foreign countries would come to America's aid. In Great Britain, American independence would "raise such a storm against the measures of [Parliament] as will...throw the kingdom into confusion." When the vote came in the congress to declare independence, Adams spoke passionately for several hours. His arguments helped persuade the representatives to declare the colonies independent.

A DIFFERENCE OF OPINION

Not everyone who supported independence welcomed *Common Sense*. John Adams thought that Paine had the wrong idea for the new kind of government that America should have. Paine's work, he said, would "do more mischief, in dividing the friends of liberty, than all the [Loyalist] writings together." Years later, however, Adams wrote, "I know not whether any man in the world has had more influence on its inhabitants or affairs for the last thirty years than Tom Paine."

Famous Figures

THOMAS PAINE
(1737–1809)

In 1774, Thomas Paine arrived in Philadelphia from England. His Quaker religious beliefs shaped his ideas on equality and the best kind of political system for America. Paine quickly joined the Patriot cause. After writing *Common Sense*, he traveled with Washington's troops as a journalist. In a series of papers called *The American Crisis*, he tried to boost the Continental Army's spirits during the darkest days of the Revolution. Paine traveled to Europe in 1787 and continued writing about politics and society. Most of his ideas, however, were rejected by the wealthy and powerful people of the day. Paine returned to America in 1802 and died an unpopular man, despite his earlier service to the country.

COMMON SENSE;

ADDRESSED TO THE

INHABITANTS

OF

AMERICA,

On the following interesting

SUBJECTS.

I. Of the Origin and Design of Government in general, with concise Remarks on the English Constitution.

II. Of Monarchy and Hereditary Succession.

III. Thoughts on the present State of American Affairs.

IV. Of the present Ability of America, with some miscellaneous Reflections.

Man knows no Master save creating HEAVEN,
Or those whom choice and common good ordain.
THOMSON.

PHILADELPHIA;
Printed, and Sold, by R. BELL, in Third-Street.
MDCCLXXVI.

Arguments against Independence

When Benjamin Franklin discussed declaring independence in 1775, Thomas Jefferson said that the Continental Congress was "revolted at it." Most Americans still saw themselves as British citizens. The British system of government, they believed, was the best in the world. The war was a result of bad decisions made in Parliament, not a basic problem with British-American relations.

Many people also wondered what kind of government an independent America would have. Abigail Adams, wife of John Adams, asked him, "Will not ten thousand difficulties arise in the formation of [an independent country]?... How shall we be governed so as to retain our liberties?" Abigail Adams also noted that most people tend to like "ancient customs and regulations"; starting a new government could be a frightening notion.

Abigail Adams, the wife of John Adams, was unusually informed and outspoken about politics for a woman of her time. In letters to her husband, she discussed many questions about the prospect of independence and even raised the subject of what women's roles would be in the new nation.

People opposed to independence reacted strongly to Paine's *Common Sense*. William Smith, a Pennsylvania minister, wrote a series of articles against it, as did Charles Inglis, another minister. They and others listed many reasons why America should not cut off its relationship with Great Britain. Smith said that forming alliances with foreign countries, such as France, was more dangerous than repairing relations with Great Britain. France lacked the military strength to aid America and, in the past, had not honored its treaties with other countries. Also, religion played a part in Smith's thinking. Like most Americans of the time, he was a Protestant. France was largely Roman Catholic. The difference in religion made many Americans suspicious of France and the help that it might offer the United States.

In his writing, Inglis argued for reconciliation. He said that Americans and Britons were united by "endearing ties," including religion and family relations. He also argued that the war was damaging the American economy. Reconciliation, he said, would boost the colonies' farming, trade, and industry. By remaining in the British Empire, American ships would receive the protection of the powerful British navy. Independence would lead to "the greatest confusion and most violent convulsions" as the war worsened.

In Their Own Words

Here is a small part of Thomas Paine's *Common Sense*.

I challenge the warmest advocate of reconciliation to [show] a single advantage that this continent can reap by being connected with Great-Britain. I repeat the challenge, not a single advantage is derived.... But the injuries and disadvantages we sustain by that connection are without number, and our duty to mankind at large, as well as to ourselves, [instructs] us to renounce the alliance.

In the Continental Congress, members who opposed declaring independence included James Rutledge, Robert Livingston, and John Dickinson. Rutledge hoped to delay a vote on independence for months, if possible. He believed that the colonies were not truly united and that it was too early to declare independence. The others shared this view. They, unlike people such as Smith and Inglis, did not think that reconciliation was possible. Still, they were not ready to take the huge step of cutting all ties with Great Britain.

In the end, Rutledge did vote for the Declaration of Independence. Livingston and Dickinson did not, though they remained loyal to the Patriot cause. The strongest voices against independence did not hold enough power in the colonies to stop the declaration.

In Their Own Words

On July 1, 1776, John Dickinson spoke against the resolution calling for independence. Here is part of one version of what he said.

I know the name of liberty is dear to each one of us; but have we not enjoyed liberty even under the English monarchy? Shall we this day renounce that to go and seek it in I know not what form of republic?... We have presented ourselves in all the ports and in all the cities of the globe, not as Americans, a people scarcely heard of, but as English. Under the shadow of this respected name, every port was open to us...every demand was heard with favor. From the moment when our separation shall take place, everything will assume a contrary direction.

CHAPTER TEN

The Articles of Confederation

WHAT

The United States creates its first official government.

ISSUE

The powers of Congress and its relation with the states.

WHERE

Philadelphia and York, Pennsylvania

WHEN

1776–1777

*W*hen the First Continental Congress met in September 1774, many Americans were upset with British policies that limited their rights. The congress gave them a way to share ideas about how to solve their problems with Great Britain. Every colony except Georgia elected delegates to go to the congress in Philadelphia, Pennsylvania. The colonies had not set up a committee or held a convention to decide how the congress would operate. Instead, the delegates decided among themselves the basic rules that they would follow. The members elected a president and said that each colony's delegation would have one vote on any issue.

At the beginning of the Second Continental Congress in May 1775, the delegates took on more powers usually held by a national government. By then, the American Revolution (1775–1783) had broken out in Massachusetts. The congress reacted by creating a Continental Army, with George Washington as its commander. The congress also spoke for the colonies as they made their last effort to prevent a larger war and remain in the British Empire.

During 1775, several members of the congress wrote documents outlining an official national government for the colonies. Silas Deane of Connecticut believed that some kind of official union would help the colonies get the best terms with the British if the two sides settled their differences. If, on the other hand, the colonies declared their independence, a union would eventually create "a complete and perfect American constitution."

Pennsylvania's Benjamin Franklin drafted what were called "articles of confederation." The colonies would unite in a confederation. Each colony would still control its own affairs within its borders, but the national government would manage the war and conduct foreign policy for the united colonies. The new national government would also settle disputes between the colonies. Franklin gave his plan to the Continental Congress in July, but the delegates did not consider it. Some members of the congress still hoped that the colonies could settle their differences with Great Britain and remain part of its empire.

Creating the Articles of Confederation

By June 1776, most members of the Continental Congress realized that the colonies could not solve their problems with Great Britain. The colonies now considered themselves states, and Richard Henry Lee of Virginia said that the states should declare their independence. Lee also proposed that the states create "a plan of confederation." On June 12, the congress formed a committee to draft articles of confederation. John Dickinson of Pennsylvania emerged as the committee leader, and he wrote the first draft of the document outlining the proposed new government.

Dickinson had to balance the powers of the new national government with the powers of the individual state governments. He wanted the confederation to play a key role in addressing problems that arose between states. The new national government would also continue the Continental Congress's role of running the war and conducting foreign policy. The confederation, however, would not have any power to directly tax the citizens of the states. It could only request that each state pay a set amount of taxes to help the new government carry out its duties. Dickinson's draft of the articles also limited the states' rights to pass new laws restricting freedom of religion or to have permanent armies during peacetime.

The committee rejected some of Dickinson's ideas, and starting in late July, the congress as a whole debated how to modify his plan. The delegates debated several key issues, such as how much power the new government should have, how members of the new congress would vote, and how to decide the amount of money that each state would contribute to the government. The members disagreed on what to do with unsettled western lands that several states claimed belonged to them. In early August, William Williams of Connecticut noted, "We make slow progress...as every inch of ground is disputed." Still, the delegates realized how important it was to have some kind of confederation. Samuel Chase of Maryland wrote that without confederation, "we shall remain weak, distracted, and divided in our councils."

The ongoing Revolution affected how the congress did its business, including approving the articles. In December, fearing a British invasion of Philadelphia, the delegates moved to Baltimore, Maryland. They returned to Philadelphia in March 1777 but fled the city again in September, when the British attacked. The debate on the articles continued in York, Pennsylvania, where the congress met until June 1778.

PART-TIME MEMBERS

Members of the Continental Congress frequently left the sessions during the debates on the Articles of Confederation and other issues. John Dickinson, for example, left Philadelphia after finishing his draft of the articles. While the congress met in Baltimore, only about half of the elected members attended. Many delegates believed that political problems in their home states were more important than the congress's work. Others had business interests that called them away. The congress had no rules enforcing attendance, and poor attendance in the congress remained a problem through the 1780s.

Slow Process for Approval

In November 1777, after making many changes to the document submitted by Dickinson's committee, the Continental Congress finally approved the Articles of Confederation. The new country was officially called the United States of America, and the Continental Congress was renamed the United

States in Congress Assembled. The states formed "a firm league of friendship," with each state keeping its "sovereignty, freedom, and independence." The states also kept all rights and powers not specifically given to the new government.

Congress then sent the Articles of Confederation to the states for their approval. Each state had to accept the articles for them to go into effect. By the spring of 1779, every state but Maryland had accepted the articles. The issue of western lands delayed Maryland's approval. Maryland, unlike Virginia and several other states, did not have any land claims in the West. Maryland insisted that the power to control those lands should be given to the new government, not to the states that claimed them. Eventually, the "landed" states agreed to give the national government the right to control the western lands. In February 1781, Maryland finally approved the articles.

The new government met for the first time in Philadelphia on March 2, 1781. Congress was the only branch of the government. It had the power to make laws, but it had no way to force the states to follow them. The articles did not create any national court system, as the U.S. Constitution later did. Congress also did not have the power to collect direct taxes from individuals or force the states to pay the taxes that they owed the national government. The final articles created a weaker government than the one that Dickinson had wanted. After the Revolution was won, some American leaders saw that the national government had to have more power if the United States was to survive and grow as a nation. In 1787, the Constitutional Convention was held in Philadelphia to make changes to the articles. Instead, the delegates created an entirely new government system—the one that is still used today.

Fast Fact

Maryland's anger over the western lands was aimed primarily at its neighbor, Virginia. On January 2, 1781, Virginia offered to give the national government land that it claimed west of the Ohio River, ending Maryland's refusal to sign the Articles of Confederation.

The new American government established under the Articles of Confederation met for the first time in March 1781 at Philadelphia's State House, later called Independence Hall. By 1787, this would be the scene of the Constitutional Convention, at which delegates sought to replace the articles with a stronger framework of government.

One Vote or Many?

The debate in Congress over the Articles of Confederation focused on three main issues. The first was how many votes in Congress to give to each state. In the Continental Congresses, each state sent a varying number of delegates, but each delegation had just one vote. States with larger populations complained about this system. They believed that each state should have a number of votes based on its population or the amount of money that it contributed to Congress. John Adams of Massachusetts and Benjamin Franklin both agreed that a state's population should determine how many votes it received. Franklin argued that the larger states would pay more to support the union, so they should have greater input into how the government was run.

The small states, however, feared that just a handful of larger states could control the government if voting was based on population. "If an equal vote be refused," said John Witherspoon of New Jersey, "the smaller states will become [servants] to the larger." Some delegates from the small states also argued that the articles were creating a union of states, not a national government that ruled over all the citizens of America. Since each state in the proposed confederation was equal, each should have the same vote in Congress.

The delegates eventually stayed with the one-state, one-vote system. As a partial compromise, certain issues, such as declaring war or raising money for defense, would require nine votes to pass. On these special issues, a group of small or large states could not decide the result on their own. In all other cases, a simple majority of seven would be enough.

Fast Fact

Samuel Chase suggested a compromise on voting in the articles. For issues regarding money, the vote would be based on each state's population. On all other issues, each state would have one vote. Congress did not act on his suggestion.

How to Raise Money?

The delegates also strongly disagreed on how Congress should raise money. Dickinson's plan called for each state to pay a share of taxes based on its total population, not counting Native Americans. That formula upset the Southern states, which had many more slaves than the Northern states did. Some Southern delegates said that the share should be based on the white population only. To slave owners, slaves were property, not people, and since other property was not being considered for this tax, slaves should not be either.

In August 1776, Congress voted to accept the taxation article as Dickinson had written it. The matter, however, came up again the next year. Southern states backed a plan to tax all lands and the improvements made to them. The idea of taxing all kinds of property was also discussed. New England states still backed Dickinson's original plan, which based the tax on total population.

New Englanders opposed the tax on land because, in general, their land was more valuable than the land in other colonies. They would end up paying more than if the tax were based on population. Some delegates also thought that slaves should be counted as property, if property was used as the basis for the tax. Nathaniel Folsom of New Hampshire said that the slaves were "one third part of the wealth of the Southern states." Some Southerners, however, agreed with Thomas Lynch Jr., of South Carolina. He said, "If it is debated whether...slaves are...property, there is an end of the confederation." In the end, the Southern states got their way, and the tax was based on the value of land.

The Western Lands

The issue of western land claims took the longest to solve. The so-called landless states without claims were Maryland, Pennsylvania, Delaware, Rhode Island, and New Jersey. Royal charters, the grants from the English kings that had established the colonies, set fixed borders for these states. The landed states had charters that let them claim land as far west as the Pacific Ocean.

Some delegates from landless states argued that the landed states could not manage so much land and that no one had realized how far away the Pacific was when the charters were written. These arguments, however, did not have a strong legal foundation. In general, the land issue came down to money. Speculators in the landless states had little chance of making as much money as landed-state speculators. The speculators made money when they bought western land at a low price and later sold it to settlers for a profit. The large land claims also meant that the landed states had an easy way to raise money to pay their taxes—they simply sold some of the land. The landless states, which did not have that option, might have a harder time paying their share of taxes.

Dickinson's original draft of the articles gave control of the western lands to the national government. During the debates in Congress, Virginia led the battle to limit national control over state land claims and won. The final document said that the new government could not set western boundaries for the states. Maryland, however, did not stop fighting the landed states. It refused to approve the articles until all the landed states volunteered to cede their claims to the national government.

The delegates went back and forth on the three main issues, and others as well. The debates were not recorded. Only the notes and letters that some of the delegates wrote give historians any information on the debates. In the end, however, the delegates were ready to compromise on most issues. As Charles Carroll of Maryland wrote, they believed that "an imperfect and somewhat unequal confederacy is better than none."

In Their Own Words

After writing the Articles of Confederation, Congress sent a letter to the states explaining why they should approve the new government. Here is part of that letter.

Let [the articles] be candidly reviewed under a sense of the difficulty of combining, in one general system, the various sentiments and interests of a continent divided into so many sovereign and independent communities.... Let them be adjusted with the temper and magnanimity of wise and patriotic legislators, who, while they are concerned for the prosperity of their own more immediate circle, are capable of rising superior to local attachments, when they may be incompatible with the safety, happiness, and glory of the general confederacy.

In Their Own Words

The Ninth Article of Confederation spelled out many specific powers given to Congress. One strong critic of the finished articles, Thomas Burke of North Carolina, believed that many parts of this article were unfair to the states. Here is part of what he wrote.

The United States ought to be as one sovereign with respect to foreign powers, in all things that relate to war or where the states have one common interest. But in all commercial or other peaceful [affairs], they ought to be as separate sovereigns.

The first is necessary, because no one can be defended from the evils of war but by the united force of all....

The second is necessary, in order that each may acquire strength to as great a degree as its circumstances may admit, without being subject to restraints which may arise from the jealousy of its neighbors.

CHAPTER ELEVEN

The Constitutional Convention

WHAT

Politicians call a convention to create
a new national government for the United States.

ISSUE

The form and powers of the new government

WHERE

Philadelphia, Pennsylvania

WHEN

1787

After Congress declared American independence in 1776, the representatives knew that they needed some form of central government to conduct war and relations with foreign countries. At the time, the thirteen states were almost like separate nations linked by a common goal—defeating the British. Few people saw the "united states" as one country with one set of laws that applied everywhere. Political leaders wanted each state's government to control its own affairs. Many people feared that a strong national government would soon become tyrannical, as they argued that Parliament, the British lawmaking body, and King George III had become.

Fast Fact

Samuel Huntington of Connecticut was the first president of Congress under the Articles of Confederation. He served from March 2, 1781, until July 6, 1781.

In 1777, Congress passed the Articles of Confederation, which created a national government, but one with weak powers. It consisted of only one body, the Congress, officially known as "the United States in Congress Assembled." Congress elected a president, but this person did not have any powers outside of Congress. The government could not directly collect taxes or control trade between the states. It also had no way to force the states to obey the laws that it passed. The new government had no court system. Its main duty was to fight in the American Revolution (1775–1783).

Each state had to approve the Articles of Confederation before they took effect. The last vote, from Maryland, came in 1781, and the new Congress met for the first time on March 2. Each state had one vote, though each sent at least two representatives to Congress. The states decided on their own how to choose these representatives. To amend, or change, the articles, every state had to agree. Most other decisions were made by a majority vote.

Problems with the Articles

Almost as soon as the articles were approved, some Americans thought that the new central government was too weak. Alexander Hamilton led the effort to reconsider the articles. He was most concerned about Congress not being able to collect taxes or regulate trade. Hamilton wanted what he called a "federal republic": the states should be part of one country with a strong central government. Each state would give up some power to this government, yet still have its own laws and control local affairs. A federal republic, Hamilton wrote in 1782, had "something noble and magnificent," compared to the "petty states, with the appearance of union only" created under the articles.

For the next several years, Congress tried to function as a national government. The limits that it faced under the articles, however, made this difficult. The country had debts from the war and needed money to carry out new business, but the states had their own debts and expenses. They did not always contribute to Congress what they were supposed to, yet they refused to give the national government the power to raise money on its own.

Congress also did not have the power to enforce some of the requirements of the Treaty of Paris, which had ended the American Revolution in 1783. Under the treaty, the states were supposed to repay old debts to Great Britain. Some states, however, made it hard for the British to collect these debts. In response, the British remained in forts along the western edges of the United States, even though they had agreed to leave them after the war. Congress did not have the ability to raise an army that could force the British out, and it lacked the power to make the states pay their debts.

By the mid-1780s, many Americans were facing tough economic times. Farmers were the hardest hit, as many owed money that they could not repay. In western Massachusetts, farmers marched to Springfield to protest the debts and rising taxes. The protesters tried to take over the federal arsenal, where weapons were stored. Local militia fired their guns and cannons to drive off the farmers. Protests in other towns also turned violent.

At first, Massachusetts asked Congress to send an army to end the rebellion. As usual, Congress had trouble raising the money to respond quickly. In the end, Massachusetts was able to settle the conflict on its own, but the violence raised the fear of rebellions in other states. More Americans saw a need for a stronger national government to keep order and defend property.

Famous Figures

ALEXANDER HAMILTON
(1755–1804)

Alexander Hamilton was born on the Caribbean island of Nevis. He came to the United States in 1772 and soon joined the Patriot cause. (Patriots were colonists who opposed British efforts to limit American freedom.) For about half of the Revolution, he served as one of George Washington's most trusted aides. Hamilton entered politics after the war, becoming a leader of the movement to create a strong national government. After the Constitutional Convention, his writings outlined the strengths of the new government. These articles, along with ones by James Madison and John Jay, are known as *The Federalist Papers*. Hamilton served as the first U.S. secretary of the treasury. He died after a duel with Aaron Burr, who at the time was the vice president.

The Call for
a Convention

Even before the uprising in Massachusetts, some politicians wanted to discuss forming a new government. George Washington, John Jay, and James Madison were among these leaders. In 1786, Washington wrote to Jay that Congress's requests for money were "actually little better than a jest" and that state governments "will laugh in your face" if you accuse them of breaking the agreements in the Treaty of Paris.

That summer, Virginia called for a convention of all the states to discuss amending the Articles of Confederation. Held in Annapolis, Maryland, the convention attracted delegates from just five states. Madison then suggested that another convention should be held the next spring in Philadelphia, Pennsylvania. After the violence in Massachusetts and smaller protests in other states, more politicians saw the need for the convention. In May 1787, delegates from every state except Rhode Island began gathering in Philadelphia.

Fast Fact

In 1787, Rhode Island's political leaders tended to favor the interests of debtors—people who owed money. The leaders feared that if a more powerful central government were created at the Constitutional Convention, it would pass laws that harmed debtors. For that reason, Rhode Island did not send delegates to Philadelphia.

The delegates elected George Washington to serve as president of the convention. He did not take part in the debates, but the other delegates knew that he supported the creation of a strong federal government. Other leading figures at the convention were Benjamin Franklin, Hamilton, and Madison. The delegates voted not to record their debates so they could talk freely without worrying about offending voters at home. Many delegates, however, took their own notes on the debates or recorded the events in their diaries.

Fast Fact

Only thirty-eight delegates signed the Constitution, although thirty-nine names appear on it. George Read of Delaware signed for John Dickinson, also of Delaware. Dickinson had left the convention because of illness.

Madison had written a proposed constitution before coming to Philadelphia. The delegates debated his plan and made changes to it. The new government that emerged was vastly different from the old one under the Articles of Confederation. On September 17, thirty-nine delegates approved the Constitution. Now the supporters of the new federal government had to convince at least nine of the thirteen states to ratify, or approve, the document. Few of the signers thought that the new government was perfect, but many probably agreed with Nicholas Gilman of New Hampshire: "[Despite] its imperfections," he wrote, "on the adoption of it depends...whether or no we shall become a respectable nation, or a people torn to pieces."

As president of the Constitutional Convention, George Washington did not take part in the debates that raged among the delegates, but he did vote on many of their resolutions. Washington was unanimously elected to lead the convention in 1787, just as he had been unanimously elected to lead the forces in the Revolution twelve years earlier.

Debating the Virginia Plan

James Madison came to the convention with a plan for how to shape the new government. This was later called the Virginia Plan. Madison wanted the government to have three parts, or branches. The legislative branch, Congress, would have two houses, an "upper" and a "lower." The executive branch would carry out the laws passed by the legislative branch. The judicial branch would make sure that the laws were carried out fairly.

Madison's plan also called for voters in the states to directly elect their representatives for the lower house of the legislature. In the past, the state legislatures chose who would represent the states in national assemblies. Madison wanted the number of legislators to be based on each state's population, as well. They would vote as individuals. This system would replace the one-state, one-vote arrangement under the Articles of Confederation.

What Madison suggested went far beyond amending the articles, and most delegates favored the broad idea of creating a new national government. George Read of Delaware said that he "was against patching up the old federal system." In one of the first votes taken, the delegates accepted the idea of a legislative branch with two houses. However, some did not accept having voters directly elect the representatives of the lower house. Roger Sherman of Connecticut said that the people "[lack] information and are constantly liable to be misled." Madison argued that "the popular election of one branch of the national legislature is essential to every plan of free government."

Delegates also disagreed on another key point. The smaller states, such as New Jersey and Connecticut, feared losing power if the old system was changed. Under the Virginia Plan, the number of representatives sent to the legislature would be based on a state's population. Issues would be decided by a vote of each

Fast Fact

As the delegates debated the workings of the legislature, they also considered the executive branch. Madison's original plan did not specify how many people would lead this branch. The delegates finally decided that it would be one person, in a position that was later called the presidency.

individual representative. In theory, larger states with more representatives could control the results of some votes. William Paterson of New Jersey said that if the larger states had more votes, "their ambition will be proportionally increased, and the small states will have every thing to fear."

Debating the New Jersey Plan

By mid-June, the delegates still disagreed on several parts of Madison's plan. Paterson then introduced a new plan for the delegates to consider. In general, this plan, known as the New Jersey Plan, addressed the concerns of the smaller states. The new government would keep its current legislative system: one house, with each state having one vote. The New Jersey Plan also limited the national government's ability to pass laws on national issues. It did, however, address the key concern of giving the national government power to collect taxes, and it created three branches of government, as in the Virginia Plan.

In Their Own Words

Here is some of William Paterson's argument for the New Jersey Plan.

It is urged that two branches in the Legislature are necessary. Why? for the purpose of a check [on power]. But the reason of the precaution is not applicable to this case. Within a particular state...such a check may be necessary. In such a body as Congress it is less necessary, and besides, the delegations of the different states are checks on each other. Do the people at large complain of Congress? No, what they wish is that Congress may have more power. If the power now proposed be not enough, the people hereafter will make additions to it.

James Madison.

In Their Own Words

One of James Madison's complaints about the New Jersey Plan rested on how Congress and the states would conduct foreign relations. Here are some of his thoughts.

Will [the New Jersey Plan] prevent those violations of the law of nations and of treaties which if not prevented must involve us in...foreign wars? The tendency of the states to these violations has been manifested in [many] instances.... The existing confederacy does not sufficiently provide against this evil. The proposed amendment to it does not [correct this]. It leaves the will of the states as uncontrolled as ever.

The supporters of a strong national government quickly attacked the New Jersey Plan. James Wilson of Pennsylvania argued that the citizens of the states wanted a stronger national government to solve current problems. "It is from the national councils," he said, "that relief is expected." Paterson said that he had been sent to Philadelphia to improve the Articles of Confederation, not to create a strong, new national government.

The Great Compromise

After several days of debate, the larger states and several smaller states from the South won a vote to focus on the Virginia Plan, not the New Jersey Plan. The issue of how many representatives the states would have and how they would vote was still unsolved. Finally, a committee came up with a compromise. In the lower house, each state's number of representatives would be based on its population. In the upper house, all the states would have the same number of representatives. The lower house members would be directly elected by the people, while state legislatures would choose the members of the upper house. The lower house would also be the only house that could introduce bills relating to taxes and spending. The upper house, however, would still vote on those bills.

Madison and a few others did not like this "Great Compromise," but in the end, delegates from most states accepted it. The debates continued for several more weeks as the delegates shaped the executive and judicial branches. At last, most of the delegates accepted the new government created in Philadelphia. But the battle over the Constitution was just beginning, because now it had to go to the states to be ratified before it could take effect.

Fast Fact

The Great Compromise is also sometimes called the Connecticut Compromise. Roger Sherman of that state first suggested the idea of giving each legislative house a different system of representation.

CHAPTER TWELVE

Ratification of the Constitution

WHAT

The states approve the U.S. Constitution.

ISSUE

Whether the government created under the Constitution was the best for the United States

WHERE

Nationwide

WHEN

1787–1790

In 1787, the delegates at the Constitutional Convention debated the form of the new American government. Almost all agreed that the old Articles of Confederation had been too weak. Some wanted a strong central government and insisted that Congress be given the power to tax, which it had lacked under the articles. Other delegates, however, wanted to preserve the power of the states as much as possible, even though they realized that the articles needed to change.

In the end, the delegates created what is called a federal government. It had some features of the old government, which was a confederation. Under the articles, Congress could not collect taxes or control trade between the states. It also had no way to force the states to obey the laws that it passed. With the old system, the lawmakers in each state, not the people directly, chose who represented the states in Congress. The new U.S. government, as outlined in the Constitution at the time, kept the same method for choosing members of the Senate, which was the "upper" house of the new Congress.

The Constitution then added a new element, letting people directly elect representatives to the House of Representatives, the "lower" house of Congress. James Madison, the main author of the Constitution, said that this system was "a clear principle of free government." The Constitution created a government that reflected the interests of the people, as well as the states.

Under the new system, the states and the national government would share some powers, such as raising taxes. Other powers, such as controlling local education and police, would be held just by the states. The national government also had some power of its own, such as declaring war and issuing money.

Fast Fact

In the late eighteenth century, the term *federal* applied to the kind of government created under the Articles of Confederation— a union of largely independent states. During the debate over the Constitution, the term took on the broader meaning of a strong national government. During the 1790s, the first political party in the United States was the Federalist Party.

The new government had three branches. The legislative branch (Congress) made the laws, the executive branch (the president) carried out the laws, and the judicial branch (the courts) made sure that the laws were fairly enforced. In Madison's thinking, the three branches would share power to ensure that one branch did not dominate the others. This separation of powers was also referred to as "checks and balances." Each branch could check, or limit, the power of the other two—keeping the power of the three branches in balance.

The Drive to Ratify

In the end, the delegates had to compromise to create the new government. Finally, on September 17, the delegates signed their names to the Constitution. The next step was for each state to call a convention to debate the Constitution and vote on whether or not to accept it. Nine out of the thirteen states had to ratify, or approve, the document to make it official. In each state, supporters of the Constitution were called federalists. Their opponents were called anti-federalists. The anti-federalists hoped to reject the Constitution altogether. If they could not, they hoped to change it to protect the rights of individuals and the states against the increased power of the new federal government.

During the Constitutional Convention, some of the anti-federalists had argued that the Constitution should have a bill of rights. Most states had such a list of basic rights that the government could not limit. They included such rights as freedom of speech, freedom of religion, and trial by jury in court cases. George Mason, who had drafted a bill of rights for Virginia's constitution, led the call for a national bill of rights. He had refused to sign the Constitution because it did not have one. As the states debated the new government structure, a number of them called for adding a bill of rights and making other amendments, or changes.

Representatives of both sides wrote newspaper articles to influence the ratification vote. The leading writers for the federalists were Madison and Alexander Hamilton. They wrote a series of pro-Constitution articles for a New York newspaper. John Jay wrote several as well. Later, these articles were collected and published as *The Federalist Papers*. Anti-federalists fought back with their own arguments. One series of essays directly challenged the ideas in *The Federalist Papers*. It was probably written by Robert Yates, who had left the Constitutional Convention to protest the new national government taking shape.

The first state to vote on the Constitution was Delaware. In December 1787, delegates at the state convention voted unanimously for the document. New Jersey and Georgia soon followed with their own unanimous votes. Pennsylvania ratified during this time. Federalist forces there had acted quickly to call a convention, before the anti-federalists could organize against the Constitution. Connecticut, a strong federalist state, gave its approval in January 1788.

> *Fast Fact*
>
> Delaware's position as the first state to ratify the Constitution led to its nickname— "the First State."

The vote to ratify was close in Massachusetts. Elbridge Gerry was one of several important political leaders in the state who opposed the Constitution. However, the anti-federalists suffered a defeat when two well-known political leaders, Samuel Adams and John Hancock, joined the federalist side. The federalists won by about twenty votes, but their opponents were able to include nine proposed amendments to the Constitution.

Maryland and South Carolina voted next to ratify, bringing the number to eight. Both sides then turned their attention to New York and Virginia. Those two states were large and wealthy. Their approval of the new government was important to ensure its survival. In Virginia, the federalists won by just ten votes, making it the tenth state to ratify. New Hampshire won the honor of clinching the approval on June 21, five days before the Virginia vote.

In New York, Hamilton faced a tough struggle against well-organized anti-federalists, but after the New York delegates learned that Virginia had ratified, they voted to ratify. Still, the vote was tight (thirty to twenty-seven), and the anti-federalists won approval of thirty-two proposed amendments to reshape the Constitution. They voted that a second convention should be held for that purpose.

On July 26, 1788, New Yorkers held a parade to celebrate the ratification of the Constitution. Having worked hard in support of the Constitution, New Yorker Alexander Hamilton was the hero of the day and rode on a float in the form of a ship named in his honor.

The Bill of Rights

The call for amendments and a second convention convinced many federalists that they should accept a bill of rights. Madison had at first opposed it, but he may have been persuaded by Thomas Jefferson to change his mind. Jefferson told Madison, "A bill of rights is what the people are entitled to against every government on earth." Madison also saw that adding a bill of rights would win support for ratification among some anti-federalists.

In 1789, while serving in the new House of Representatives, Madison went over the amendments submitted by the different states. He then gave Congress a list of possible amendments. Congress approved twelve of these and sent them to the states to ratify. The states ratified ten out of the twelve amendments, and these became known as the Bill of Rights.

The Anti-Federalists' Complaints

The anti-federalists had many arguments against the Constitution. One complaint was that the new government was not truly republican. To the political thinkers of the day, a republican government was the best available. Voters elected representatives who reflected their interests and desires. The representatives were supposed to know the voters well and represent a small community. The new U.S. government, the anti-federalists argued, required each member of the House to represent too many voters. In general, they claimed, the country was too big to have a national republican government that could respond to the voters' needs.

Republican beliefs suggested that a strong central power could lead to a tyranny. The anti-federalists did not want to give Congress control of the state militia, as the Constitution called for. They also feared large standing, or permanent, armies, which the new government was allowed to form. One writer warned that "an army will subvert the forms of the government under whose authority they are raised, and establish one according to the pleasure of their leader." Other anti-federalists noted that the colonies had won their independence without a standing army.

Some anti-federalists believed that the new federal system took too much power from the states and the people and gave it to Congress—especially the Senate—and the executive branch. The anti-federalists believed that senators and the president might use that power for their own financial gain or to rule as tyrants. Many anti-federalists thought that this power given to the new national government would lead to a small, powerful group of men running the country. The American Revolution (1775–1783), they argued, had been fought to end the rule of just a few people over the many.

Other specific criticisms included the lack of a trial by jury in civil cases (lawsuits between individuals). The Constitution only allowed jury trials in criminal cases. Some anti-federalists also did not like giving Congress the power to collect taxes. Pennsylvania anti-federalists said that this power let

Fast Fact

Three states— Georgia, Connecticut, and Massachusetts— did not ratify the Bill of Rights at the time. Georgia and Connecticut claimed that it was unnecessary, while Massachusetts lawmakers could not agree on which amendments to accept. The three states finally ratified the Bill of Rights in 1939, to honor the one hundred fiftieth anniversary of the Constitution and the year that Congress first proposed a Bill of Rights.

Congress "command the whole, or any part of the property of the people." That power, along with others granted to Congress, took away power from the states.

In Their Own Words

Here's a selection from an article that was probably by Robert Yates, a leading New York anti-federalist.

This government is to possess absolute and uncontrollable power...with respect to every object to which it extends.... Some small degree of power is still left to the states, but a little attention to the powers vested in the general government will convince every candid man, that if it is capable of being [carried out], all that is reserved for the individual states must very soon be annihilated.... It has authority to make laws which will affect the lives, liberty, and property of every man in the United States.

Defending the Constitution

On the whole, the federalists were more active than the anti-federalists in the debate over the Constitution. They wrote more articles and moved quickly to gain support at the state conventions. The federalists also focused on issues that could win wide national support and appealed to Americans' pride. The Constitution, they argued, would make the United States stronger and allow it to compete with other countries in foreign trade.

One key argument for the Constitution was that the previous government had been so weak. Even anti-federalists admitted this, yet they refused to give the new government the power needed to fix the problems. The weakness under the Articles of Confederation, Hamilton wrote, stemmed from "fundamental errors in [their] structure." Only a completely new system, as outlined in the Constitution, would correct those errors.

On the issue of having a republican government for a large country, Madison argued that bigger could actually be better. In any government, he said, groups or factions emerge that work to promote their own interests. In a small republic, it would be easy for a group to win a majority and force its policies on the whole. However, in a larger republican government with more factions, it is "less probable that a majority of the whole will have a common motive to invade the rights of other citizens." The interests of the competing groups would check their power, just as the different branches of government checked one another's power.

Madison also examined the states' supposed loss of power. The anti-federalists, he said, focused on the states but forgot that the people held the power in both the state and the national governments. The two forms of government were not competing; they merely had different powers in their jobs of serving the people. Since the state governments were closer to the people, they would actually have more power to influence voters in any disagreement between the states and the national government.

In one of his articles, Hamilton tackled the issue of standing armies. He noted that the states faced potential enemies, since Great Britain and Spain controlled neighboring territories. Settlers on the American frontier also faced threats from Native Americans. The dangers, Hamilton wrote, were common, and the defense should be handled by the national government, not by individual states.

The federalists believed that the Constitution ended the weakness of the old confederation while still protecting liberty. Hamilton admitted that the new government was not perfect, but then neither were the men who had created it.

Fast Fact

During the debate over ratifying the Constitution, British troops were stationed on American soil, even though the British had previously agreed to leave their forts along the western frontier.

John Jay,
about 1810.

In Their Own Words

In an article written in April 1788, John Jay urged New Yorkers to ratify the Constitution. Here is some of what he wrote.

The men who formed this plan...do not hold it up as the best of all possible ones, but only as the best which they could unite in and agree [to].... You cannot but be sensible that this plan or constitution will always be in the hands and power of the people, and that if on experiment it should be found defective or incompetent, they may either remedy its defects or substitute another in its [place].

Glossary

allies—friends and supporters of a person or country

amendment—a change or addition to a legal document

ammunition—bullets and shells fired from guns

atonement—seeking forgiveness for an error

banished—forced to leave a community or state permanently

bill—a proposal for a new law

cede—to give up the legal right to claim territory

charter—a document from a ruler giving citizens permission to form a colony

civil—relating to a government, its citizens, and their affairs

confederation—a union of independent states

corruption—the use of illegal methods to gain money or power

delegate—a person chosen to represent others at a meeting or convention

despotism—a government system with one powerful ruler who denies citizens their freedom

factions—groups with opposing political views

federal—describing a political system in which individual states join together, giving
some powers to a central government and keeping some powers for themselves

grievance—a complaint about some-one's actions

legislature—the part of a government that makes laws

militia—a part-time military force composed of local citizen volunteers

moral—correct, as defined by religious or legal teachings

negligently—without concern for others

petition—a request to the government to carry out some action, or the actual document
making that request

pietism—an emotional form of religious expression

plantations—large farms where usually just one crop is grown for sale

radical—extreme in thoughts or actions, compared with most members of a community

ratify—to formally approve a suggested action

repeal—to overturn a law

resolution—a statement of belief or desire to take action

revival—a meeting held to help Christians deepen their faith and to convert people
to Christianity

skirmishes—limited battles between small military forces

sovereignty—the authority to govern

supernatural—not explained by science or reason

treason—any attempt to overthrow or weaken a legal government

tyranny—a government system that denies individuals their freedom

Bibliography

BOOKS

Butler, Jon. *Religion in Colonial America*. New York: Oxford University Press, 2000.

Collier, Christopher, and James Lincoln Collier. *Pilgrims and Puritans, 1620–1676*. New York: Benchmark Books, 1998.

Gaustad, Edwin S. *Roger Williams: Prophet of Liberty*. New York: Oxford University Press, 2001.

King, David. *Colonies and Revolution*. New York: John Wiley, 2003.

MacBain, Jenny. *The Salem Witch Trials*. New York: Rosen Publishing Group, 2003.

Powell, Phelan. *Governor William Berkeley: Governor of Virginia*. Philadelphia: Chelsea House, 2001.

Saari, Peggy. *Colonial America: Biographies*. 2 vols. Detroit: U.X.L., 2000.

Schultz, Eric B., Michael J. Tougias, and Craig E. Blohm. *King Philip's War*. Peterborough, NH: Cobblestone Press, 2000.

Weber, Michael. *The Young Republic*. Austin: Raintree Steck-Vaughn, 2000.

Weidner, Daniel W. *Creating the Constitution: The People and Events That Formed the Nation*. Berkeley Heights, NJ: Enslow Publishers, 2002.

Westermann, Karen T. *John Peter Zenger: Free Press Advocate*. Philadelphia: Chelsea House, 2001.

WEB SITES

The Avalon Project at Yale Law School—Documents in Law, History and Diplomacy
www.yale.edu/lawweb/avalon/avalon.htm

The History Place—American Revolution
www.historyplace.com/unitedstates/revolution/index.html

The Library of Congress—America's Story: Colonial America, 1492–1763
www.americasstory.com/cgi–bin/page.cgi/jb/colonial

The Library of Congress—Religion and the Founding of the American Republic
lcweb.loc.gov/exhibits/religion/religion.html

The United States Constitution Online *www.usconstitution.net/index.html*

Cumulative Index